Johnson gives dramatic presen ... ...c Covenant of Gra ... conflict of the two seeds. It is gripping and compelling while it illustrates the doctrinal argument with power. He tells the story that is the ontological rubric behind all good stories. Giving serious attention to Johnson's tenacious engagement with the biblical theme of *The Kingdom of God* will expand one's personal knowledge of Scripture, extend one's confidence in the wisdom and certainty of divine providence, and exact transparent and pure praise to God for his invincible grace.

—Tom Nettles

Of the many books that exist on covenant theology, rare are those that are accessible to neophytes while at the same time instructing the well read student on the subject. This one does both. If Jeff Johnson's first book, *The Fatal Flaw*, explained what Baptist covenant theology is not, *The Kingdom of God* explains what it is. In my view, the most important contribution of this work is to bring us the history of salvation through all the biblical covenants in a Reformed Baptist perspective. The deeper treatment that Johnson gives to the Abrahamic Covenant in this work is one of the clearest statements I have read. After you finish reading it, you will have a clearer view of the big picture of the kingdom of God.

—Pascal Denault

The Kingdom of God by Jeffrey Johnson is a work I commend to be read both by Baptists and Paedobaptists. He explains the biblical covenants in relationship to the kingdom of God through the whole Bible. Especially interesting is his explanation of the Abrahamic Covenant as one covenant with two elements, both unconditional and conditional. This is based upon his understanding of the continued requirement of the broken Covenant of Works as well as the instituted promise of the Covenant of Grace in Genesis 3:15. Thus, he places the Lord Jesus Christ at the center of God's covenants to reestablish the fallen kingdom of God. I found his narration of the covenants and kingdom through biblical history almost devotional as well as informative. I found my heart warmed at the faithfulness of God in biblical history to bring His Son into this world to fulfill the Covenant of Works for us and to establish the victory of the Covenant of Grace over sin, Satan, death, and hell for His chosen people. No small task for a theological work! One area of disagreement was his explanation of the Sinai Covenant as a reinstitution of the Covenant of Works. I believe that there is only one pure Covenant of Works instituted in history and that the Sinai Covenant was a subsidiary and temporary addition to the Abrahamic Covenant which proclaimed the Covenant of Works in the Law and also proclaimed Christ in the Covenant of Grace in the sacrificial system. However, Johnson did affirm the way of faith alone under the Sinai Covenant for believers like Moses, Joshua, David, etc. So, other than that quibble, I recommend the reading of *The Kingdom of God* as a welcomed addition to Baptist covenantal theology. I think you will be blessed to read his presentation of the Lord Jesus Christ as fulfilling the Covenant of Works for us that God's Grace may justly fall upon sinners.

—Fred Malone

THE KINGDOM OF GOD

THE KINGDOM OF GOD

Baptist Covenant Theology

JEFFREY D. JOHNSON

FREE GRACE PRESS

The Kingdom of God:
A Baptist Covenant Theology

Copyright © 2023 by Jeffrey D. Johnson

Published by

Free Grace Press
815 Exchange Ave., Ste. 101
Conway, AR 72032

Email: support@freegracepress.com
Website: freegracepress.com

Cover design: Scott Schaller

First printing, 2014

Revised, 2023

Printed in the United States of America

Unless otherwise noted, Scripture is taken from The Holy Bible, English Standard Version, copyright © 2001 by Crossway Bibles, a division of Good News Publishers. Used by Permission. All rights reserved.

The Scripture references marked NKJV are taken from the New King James Version. Copyright © 1982 by Thomas Nelson, Inc. Used by permission. All rights reserved.

The Scripture references marked KJV are taken from the King James Version of the Bible.

ISBN: 978-1-952599-60-6

For additional Reformed Baptist titles, please visit our website at freegracepress.com

Dedicated to

Tommy Walls

A Friend Who Loves at All Times

Contents

	Foreword	11
	Introduction	13
1.	The Dichotomous Nature of the Abrahamic Covenant	29
2.	The Wording of the Abrahamic Covenant	43
3.	Abraham's Two Seeds	53
4.	Abraham's Physical Seed	65
5.	Abraham's Spiritual Seed	87
6.	New Testament Affirmation	111
7.	The Dual Covenantal Framework of Romans	121
8.	The Separation of Law & Gospel	147
	Appendix	161
	Bibliography	165

Foreword

Jeff Johnson has given us a lot to chew on. This treatment of the covenants gives a tightly argued discussion of the relation between the Covenant of Works and the Covenant of Grace. He shows that if one relativizes the Covenant of Works then the fundamental glory of the Covenant of Grace is gone. The Covenant of Works, originally given in simple form to Adam as the Federal head of humanity, reflects the infinite and intrinsic glory and prerogative of God and shows the beauty of God's expectation of perfect righteousness from His rational, moral-based creatures. Covenants appropriate to subsequent events continue to unfold the absolutes of the Covenant of Works and also contain specific stipulations to give expression to one's relation to the Covenant of Works. Finally, it is only the Lord Jesus Christ that meets the demands of the Covenant of Works, both positively and negatively, thus bringing to bear the freedom of the Covenant of Grace for all those that repent of sin and trust exclusively in Christ as the covenant-keeper. It is He whose work will cause the knowledge of the glory of God to cover the earth.

Wending their way through the entire discussion are excellent treatments of the dichotomous nature of the covenant with Abraham, the age-long war between the seed of the woman and the seed of the Serpent, the relentless manifestations of human depravity and attempts at self-righteousness, the church as the true fulfillment of God's pledge to have a people as His own, and the theological justification for the doctrines of grace. Placed within this epic discussion of covenantal operations is the Baptist logic of what constitutes true inclusion in the New Covenant.

After the systematic and exegetical presentation of his argument, in part two Johnson gives a cover-to-cover, Genesis-to-Revelation dramatic presentation of the story of the outworking of the Covenant of Grace through the conflict of the two seeds. It is gripping and compelling while it illustrates the doctrinal argument with power. He tells the story that is the ontological rubric behind all good stories. Giving serious attention to Johnson's tenacious engagement with the biblical theme of *The Kingdom of God* will expand one's personal knowledge of Scripture, extend one's confidence in the wisdom and certainty of divine providence, and exact transparent and pure praise to God for His invincible grace.

—Tom Nettles

Introduction

Covenant theology and biblical theology are mutually interdependent. Covenant theology seeks to understand the nature and relationship between the divine covenants of redemptive history. In contrast, biblical theology seeks to understand the development of the central plotline of the biblical story. Covenant theology reminds us that God exclusively interacts with man through covenants, while biblical theology reminds us that God's covenantal dealings with man are not only progressive but also eschatological in nature. Biblical theology explains how the progressive development of redemptive history ends in the restoration of all things in Christ, while covenant theology explains how the restoration of all things has flowed out of the divine covenants that are revealed in the Old and New Testaments. Both are concerned with the development of the biblical narrative as it is rooted in the person and work of the Lord Jesus Christ. Thus, to understand covenant theology, we must understand biblical theology and vice versa.[1]

Due to the overlap between covenant theology and biblical theology, this book seeks to introduce covenant and biblical

---

[1] For a basic overview of the different methods of biblical theology, see Edward Klink and Darian Lockett, *Understanding Biblical Theology* (Grand Rapids: Zondervan, 2012).

theology from a distinct Reformed Baptist perspective. Its objective is not only to explain the relationship between the Old and New Testaments but also to elucidate the overarching storyline of the biblical narrative. Special attention is given to the kingdom motif that runs throughout the pages of Scripture.

One difficulty in discerning the storyline of the Bible is the disparity between the Old and New Testaments. There is the Old Covenant with its emphasis on law, and there is the New Covenant with its emphasis on grace. Similarly, there was the Jewish nation, which was a geopolitical entity, and there is the Christian church, which is a spiritual entity. Old Testament saints were not allowed to eat pork; however, New Testament saints often "pig out" on pork. God once said, "an eye for an eye," but He now says, "turn the other cheek."

How do we reconcile specific mandates to Israel (e.g., to destroy their enemies, to distinguish between clean and unclean animals, etc.) with the teachings of Christ, who taught His followers to bless and pray for their enemies, and who showed Peter that all animals were now clean, etc.? Moreover, how do we reconcile these and the many other general differences between the Old and New Testaments? With so much disparity, is there a unified message between the two testaments? One could safely assume the central plot of the Scriptures is the gospel, but how do all the differences between the Old and New Testaments come together to form the unified gospel message?

The question of the unity and diversity of the Old and New Testaments has baffled biblical students over the centuries, which has led to many of today's divergent theological systems of thought.[2] In response to this perplexing question, some have

---

[2] Charles Spurgeon went as far as to say, "The doctrine of the covenant lies at the root of all true theology. It has been said that he who well

sought to disregard the Old Testament altogether. The Christian Gnostics of the Patristic age are an example of thorough discontinuity. Because Christian Gnostics viewed the physical world as evil, they rejected the God of the Old Testament, who created the physical universe. In addition, because they thought the Old and New Testaments had nothing substantial in common, the somewhat invasive solution of some was to simply cut the Old Testament out of the canon of Scripture altogether.

In stark contrast, Christian Zionists seek to smooth over the differences between the Old and New Testaments, producing a complete continuity. They believe the church should seek to rebuild the Jewish Temple and reestablish the sacrificial system. For these professing Christians, being radically pro-Israeli and kosher is next to godliness. In the end, Christian Zionists, unlike the Patristic Age Gnostics, see no fundamental difference between the Old and New Testaments.

Although these are two extreme examples of how some view the relationship between the Old and New Testaments, every Bible student must draw the line somewhere. We must discern to what degree there is both discontinuity and continuity between the Old and New Testaments.

As a result, some covenantal systems stress the discontinuity while other systems stress the continuity between the two testaments. Although our goal is not to expound or analyze all the positions on the subject, the illustrative chart below will serve as a directory for some of the major views

---

understands the distinction between the Covenant of Works and the Covenant of Grace, is a master of divinity. I am persuaded that most of the mistakes which men make concerning the doctrines of Scripture are based on fundamental errors with regard to the covenants of law and grace" ("Sermon XL, The Covenant," *The Sermons of Rev. C. H. Spurgeon of London*, 9th Series, New York: Robert Carter & Brothers, 1883, p. 172).

arising from differing interpretations of the biblical covenants. Those views emphasizing the discontinuity are listed toward the left, while those emphasizing continuity are listed toward the right.

Discontinuity ⟵⟶ **Continuity**
Gnosticism
   Dispensationalism
      Progressive Dispensationalism
        Historical Premillennialism
          New Covenant Theology
            Baptist Covenant Theology
              Presbyterian Covenant Theology
                New Perspective of Paul
                  Federal Vision
                    Reconstructionism
                      Zionism

In essence, each of these theological positions is based on a particular attempt to resolve the difficulty of the discontinuity between the Old and New Testaments while seeking to maintain a unified message throughout the Scriptures.

As one can imagine, these covenantal paradigms are more than a peripheral matter. If they were of minor importance, then they would have little to no influence on the other doctrines of Scripture. Instead, like a contextual lens that provides clarity and unity to the various doctrines of the Bible, one's covenantal position functions as an interpretive framework or hermeneutical grid that shapes how one understands the individual parts of the Scriptures. In other words, one's covenantal position, whatever it may be, has the power to shape everything else that person believes about the

Scriptures.[3] For instance, one's understanding of the nature of God, the gospel, the nature and role of Israel, the nature of the church, the ordinances, and the doctrine of the end times are significantly impacted by one's understanding of the relationship between the Old and New Testaments. Herein lies the importance of correctly understanding both the continuity and discontinuity of the Old and New Testaments.

Of all the covenantal and hermeneutical systems of thought, the two most prevalent are Dispensationalism and Presbyterian covenant theology.[4] These are two contrasting systems of thought. For instance, Dispensationalists stress the discontinuity, while covenantal Presbyterians stress the continuity between the Old and New Testaments. Dispensationalists view the differences between the Old and New Testaments as being parts of two different plans of God for two distinct peoples—Israel and the Church. On the other hand, Covenantal Presbyterians blend the differences between the Old and New Testaments together and view the Jewish

---

[3] Sound hermeneutics are derived from sound theology. Conversely, sound theology is derived from sound hermeneutics. It is a common mistake to artificially presuppose a certain hermeneutical method without first studying how Scripture interprets Scripture. Sadly, many Bible students claim a certain method of interpretation without first proving that method is derived from and supported by Scripture. In other words, the authority on Biblical hermeneutics is *sola scriptura*. Therefore, just as our understanding of salvation must be derived from the Bible, our hermeneutical principles must be derived from the Bible. Once we understand that the Bible is the authority of our hermeneutics, our biblical theology cannot help but shape our biblical hermeneutics as much as our biblical hermeneutics shapes our biblical theology. This is because the many parts of Scripture are needed to understand the whole of Scripture as much as the whole of Scripture is needed to understand its parts. Thus, it is not a question of which one comes first as much as it is a matter of seeking to maintain a cohesive balance between the two.

[4] A more recent covenantal framework is New Covenant Theology. For a contemporary, comprehensive understanding of New Covenant Theology, see Peter J. Gentry's and Stephen J. Wellum's work *Kingdom through Covenant: A Biblical-Theological Understanding of the Covenants* (Wheaton, IL: Crossway, 2012).

nation and the Christian Church as virtually the same—a people of God consisting of "believers and their seed."[5]

In contrast to these two opposing systems, Baptist covenant theology, the position presented in this book, views the discontinuity between the old and New Covenants as inhering in two distinct yet vital parts of one unified gospel message which runs throughout the entirety of the Scriptures. For example, without the law of the Old Covenant, there would be no grace in the New Covenant. Without the physical seed of Abraham (i.e., Jesus Christ), there is no spiritual seed of Abraham (i.e., believers). This position sees continuity in the discontinuity of the two testaments. Without maintaining the right balance between the discontinuity of the Old and New Testaments, there is no coherent, unified gospel message.

Regardless of the particulars, the debate between continuity and discontinuity centers on the nature of the Abrahamic Covenant and the promises God made to the seed of Abraham. Was the promised seed referring to Abraham's physical seed (the Jews), Abraham's spiritual seed (the church), or both? Indeed, a misunderstanding of the nature of Abraham's two seeds and their relationship to one another has contributed to much of the theological confusion surrounding the identity of the true people of God and the nature of the relationship between the Old and New Testaments.

Presbyterian Covenant Theology

Presbyterian covenant theology is one such theological confusion. This covenantal system attempts to establish basic continuity between the physical children of Abraham in the Old Covenant and Abraham's spiritual children in the New

---

[5] See Herman Hoeksema, *Believers and Their Seed: Children in the Covenant* (Grand Rapids: Reformed Free Publishing, 1997).

Covenant. To construct continuity between the Old and New Covenants, common ground must be found between Israel and the church. This common ground is found by artificially placing the Covenant of Grace[6] outside of time and unifying the Old and New Covenants together by claiming that they are manifestations of the Covenant of Grace.[7]

In other words, the Presbyterian covenantal system is rooted in the concept that there is an overarching Covenant of Grace that stands outside of time that was progressively revealed in time through the consecutive unfolding of the various covenants of redemptive history. The Covenant of Grace was first manifested in its rudimentary form in the *protoevangelium* in Genesis 3:15. Then, it was manifested successively, with greater degrees of clarity, in the Noahic,

---

[6] The Covenant of Grace speaks of the nature of the relationship God has with believers as opposed to the "Covenant of Works," which speaks of the nature of the relationship He has with non-believers.

[7] One should note there is a theological difference between an atemporal covenant and a covenantal construct. The Covenant of Redemption, which is the eternal and covenantal plan of the Triune God to redeem humanity, is an example of an atemporal covenant. This is because the Covenant of Redemption was made before creation between the Father, Son, and Holy Spirit. The Covenant of Grace, on the other hand, is an example of a covenant construct. Although the Covenant of Grace is a part the execution of the Covenant of Redemption, it is not an atemporal covenant because it is not a covenant between the Persons of the Trinity, but rather it is a covenant between God and man. Because man is not eternal, the Covenant of Grace cannot be eternal. More precisely, the Covenant of Grace is one and the same as the New Covenant established at the death of Jesus Christ. Because Old Testament saints were saved by looking forward to the coming Messiah, it is theologically proper to speak of the Covenant of Grace as retroactively working in the Old Testament dispensation even through it was not officially established until the promulgation of the New Covenant. The Covenant of Grace actively or retroactively incorporates all believers in both the Old and New Testament periods. This is why the Covenant of Grace should be viewed as a covenant construct operating throughout redemptive history, despite its not being officially established until the death of its Federal Head – the man Christ Jesus.

Abrahamic, Mosaic, and Davidic covenants. The Covenant of Grace is finally manifested in its fullness in the New Covenant.[8]

It is important to note that none of these covenants are to be understood as distinct and separate covenants; rather, they are to be thought of as different *administrations* of the one overarching Covenant of Grace that was established by God outside of time. The thread that runs through all these administrations and ties them together is that they are all manifestations of the transhistorical and atemporal Covenant of Grace.

Infants are to be included as members of the Covenant of Grace because each administration has been consistently established with "believers and their seed." Although various nonessential elements of the Covenant of Grace were often altered with each successive administration (e.g., the Abrahamic, Mosaic, and New Covenant), the essence of the Covenant of Grace has always remained the same throughout redemptive history. As a result, there is a basic and fundamental unity between the Old and New Testaments and a single covenantal plan of redemption. The apparent discontinuity between the Old and New Covenants relates only to the unnecessary elements (accidentals) of the different administrations of the Covenant of Grace, not the covenant itself.[9]

---

[8] See chapter 14, "The Unity of the Covenant of Grace," in Robert Reymond's *A New Systematic Theology of the Christian Faith* (Nashville: Thomas Nelson Publishers, 1998), 503-544.

[9] Some within Presbyterian covenant theology have stepped closer to the Baptist position by confessing that the Mosaic Covenant is a republication of the Covenant of Works. This admission significantly advocates a higher degree of discontinuity between the old and New Covenants because the Mosaic Covenant no longer is considered a manifestation of the Covenant of Grace. But they still teach that the Abrahamic Covenant was an administration of the Covenant of Grace was established with "believers and their seed." Thus, if covenant children were brought into the Covenant of

In the end, the true people of God and the members of God's covenant people have always been a mixture of the spiritual and physical seed—"believers and their seed."

Dispensationalism

On the other end of the spectrum, Dispensationalists do not emphasize continuity; rather, they emphasize discontinuity between the Old and New Covenants. Dispensationalists teach that God has two distinct people groups: Israel (the physical seed of Abraham) and the Church (the spiritual seed of Abraham). For Dispensationalists, it is important that one does not confuse God's physical people with God's spiritual people.

Similarly, God has two distinct objectives. One objective regards the nation of Israel, while the other objective regards the church. God promised in the Old Testament to make the physical children of Abraham into a great nation through the coming Messiah who would rule upon the throne of David. According to Dispensationalists, the fulfillment of this Old Testament objective has been temporarily postponed while the Lord is building the Church—a spiritual people. Once God is finished building the Church, He will return to His original objective by fulfilling the promises to Abraham and David, which will take place in the future millennial reign of Christ.[10]

Grace in the Old Testament, then they must be included in the Covenant of Grace in the New Testament. See Bryan D Estelle, J. V. Fesko, and David VanDrunen, eds., *The Law is Not of Faith: Essays on Works and Grace in the Mosaic Covenant* (Phillipsburg, NJ: P&R, 2009).

[10] Note that Progressive Dispensationalists (a subgroup within Dispensationalism) have conceded that the church is indeed Abraham's spiritual seed. Even so, the church and Israel must remain distinct from one another.

The Common Flaw of These Two Contrasting Systems

In seeking to understand the relationship between the Old and New Testaments and the relationship between Abraham's physical and spiritual seed, Presbyterian covenant theology has sought to unify these two people groups by stating that the Covenant of Grace has been established (in both the Old and New Testaments) with believers (the spiritual seed) and their children (the physical seed). For Presbyterian covenant theology, there is a single covenantal plan of redemption that incorporates believers (who are born again by the Spirit) and their physical offspring (who are merely born of the flesh). Meanwhile, Dispensationalists have sought to keep Abraham's physical seed (the Jews) separate from Abraham's spiritual seed (the Church) by stating that God has two separate and distinct objectives for each group.

In one sense, the debate concerning the continuity and discontinuity of the Old and New Covenants centers on the true identity of the people of God and the relationship between Abraham's physical seed (the Jews) and Abraham's spiritual seed (the Church). This returns us to the original question: Who are the true children of Abraham? Are the physical offspring of Abraham the children God had in mind when He promised Abraham a seed? Or was the seed of Abraham referring to those who have the faith of Abraham? Or is the seed of Abraham a combination of believers and their physical offspring? The differing answers given to this question separate these theological positions from one another.

As we shall see, both Dispensationalism and Presbyterian covenantalism stumble at the same point. They both identify God's people as including "a physical seed" (either the unbelieving physical Jew or the unbelieving child of the believer) as belonging to the true people of God. What distinguishes Baptist covenant theology from Dispensationalism and Presbyterian covenant theology is the teaching that believers alone are and always have been the true people of God.

Additionally, Presbyterian covenant theology begins with the presupposition that the various covenants in the Old and New Testaments are merely different administrations of one overarching Covenant of Grace. Yet Presbyterian covenant theology has little to say about the ongoing revelation of the Covenant of Works. Baptist covenant theology, however, understands that salvation and justification have always belonged to the Covenant of Grace. Yet it also understands that judgment and condemnation have always come from the Covenant of Works.

The Covenant of Works did not cease after it was broken by Adam's fall; rather, it remained in operation and continues to hold fallen man captive until he is spiritually transferred, by faith alone, into the membership of the Covenant of Grace. It is vital to understand that the demands and curses of the Covenant of Works are upon all who are born of flesh, for God's law must stand over man until its penalties and demands are fully satisfied.

Baptist Covenant Theology

This leads to the Reformed Baptist position—Baptist covenant theology. This position differs from Presbyterian covenant theology in that it does not look at the various covenants of the Old Testament as administrations of the Covenant of Grace. Rather, it should be recognized that the progression of historical covenants was distinct arrangements designed to serve, foreshadow, and establish the Covenant of Grace by the work of Jesus Christ. In other words, the Covenant of Grace that was promised throughout the Old Testament could not have come to fruition in the New Covenant until the Covenant of Works was fulfilled by the life and death of Christ Jesus. Simply, the Abrahamic Covenant promised the gospel, the Mosaic Covenant explained the cost of the gospel, and the New Covenant established the gospel.

It is important to see that the gospel is revealed throughout the Old Testament. For example, the gospel burst into the historical narrative as soon as sin established the need for a Messiah (Gen. 3:1-20). Here the gospel was tied to the promised "seed." The hope of redemption and reconciliation with God was bound to the woman's offspring.

This gospel was promised to Adam and Eve and then again to Abraham. God promised Abraham that, in his physical seed, all the nations of the world would be blessed. Salvation would come through the woman's seed, and God revealed to Abraham that the promised seed would be one of his personal descendants.

Both Abraham and the believing remnant of Israel were saved by faith in the promise. They were brought into the Covenant of Grace only after they believed the promise. However, the promise was based upon a stipulation that demanded the establishment of perfect righteousness.

Without the establishment of perfect righteousness by Abraham's seed, there would be no grounds for believers to be justified by grace alone. To bring salvation to the nations, this promised seed had to fulfill all the legal demands of the Covenant of Works (Gal. 3:13, 14; 4:4, 5). In essence, the promise of the Abrahamic Covenant was that the seed of Abraham would bring blessing of salvation to the nations by keeping the law. Although the gospel was unconditionally promised to Abraham who received it by faith, Abraham's physical seed was born under the law. The legal condition of the Abrahamic Covenant required the biological children of Abraham to be circumcised. If this condition wasn't satisfied, the physical children of Abraham would be "cut off" and separated from the people of God.

As we shall see, the legal condition of the Abraham Covenant was not merely the cutting of the flesh but implied an even deeper cutting of the heart. That is, circumcision required full separation from the world and complete obedience to God from the heart, as it symbolized the removal of the old nature and the creation of a new heart.

God explained the seriousness of circumcision by establishing the Mosaic Covenant with the physical seed of Abraham. The Mosaic Covenant does not add more requirements upon Israel but simply explained with more clarity what was already required in circumcision. As the Apostle Paul explained many years later when he said circumcision requires complete obedience to the Law of Moses (Gal. 5:3). For Abraham's seed to keep the condition of the Abrahamic Covenant and to bring salvation to the nations, the seed of Abraham had to completely obey the moral law of God from the heart.

In the Garden, God promised the women that her seed would crush the Serpent's head. God promised Abraham that the seed of the woman would be one of his descendants. In time, the Davidic covenant provided additional light to God's covenantal plan of redemption. Jacob's prophetic blessing upon Judah had already eliminated the other eleven tribes of Israel as the progenitor of the promised seed. Still, the Davidic covenant further specified that the Messiah's origins would be David's son.

From that point forward, the federal head of the Jewish nation (the king[s] of Judah) was responsible for fulfilling the covenant on behalf of the nation. Otherwise, the seed of David would not be legally fit to rule and represent the people of God (Ps. 132:11-12). That is to say, the required obedience of the Covenant of Works fell upon the shoulders of one man.

The children of Adam, Abraham, and David were all born under the demands and curse of the Covenant of Works. There was not a man to be found among them who could satisfy the heavy requirements of the law. Yet despite their failure, God remained faithful to His promise, for when all hope seemed to be lost, there was a physical descendant of Abraham and David who could keep the condition of the Covenant of Works. The long-awaited promised seed had finally arrived with the birth of Jesus.

Like His fellow man, the Lord was born of a woman under the law. However, unlike His fellow man, Jesus Christ kept the law in its entirety and died under its curse as a righteous man. In so doing, Christ, the last Adam, established the spiritual blessings foreshadowed by the Abrahamic, Mosaic, and Davidic covenants by doing what the first Adam (and all his descendants) never could.

Like Abraham, who was justified by faith alone, those who believe in this particular seed, Jesus Christ, are also justified and counted among Abraham's spiritual seed by faith alone. This brings the promises and blessings of Abraham to the nations freely without obedience to the law, regardless of whether they are physically circumcised. This way, grace is open to all nations, both Jews and Gentiles. For it is not those who are born of the flesh who are united to Christ (the one and only federal head of the Covenant of Grace) but those, and only those, who are born of the Spirit.

With this covenantal framework, only believers belong to and have ever belonged to the Covenant of Grace. Yet it is important not to miss that those born in the flesh, both in the Old and New Testament periods, have all been born into a covenantal relationship with God. However, this covenantal relationship is one of law and works. As a result, everyone born of the flesh, whether Jew, Gentile, or the child of a believer, is born under the condemnation and legal demands of the Covenant of Works.

It is also important to note that the Jewish nation has been dissolved, having broken the covenant God made with them. Indeed, this is the fate deserved by all covenant-breakers. On the Day of Judgment, God will reject all covenant-breakers who remain outside of the saving union with Christ Jesus.

The only physical seed (person) who has kept the terms of the Covenant of Works in both its conditions and penalties is the Lord Jesus Christ. The blessings of the covenant are to be found in Christ alone. Christ alone is the fulfillment of the promised seed of the woman. Christ alone is the fulfillment of the Abrahamic Covenant. Christ alone is the fulfillment of the Mosaic Covenant. Christ alone is the fulfillment of the Davidic Covenant. Therefore, only by being spiritually united to Christ by faith can any person (Jew, Gentile, or child) become a true member of Abraham's spiritual family, an heir to the promised inheritance, and thus a member of the Covenant of Grace.

Our Objective

The objective of this book is to prove that the Abrahamic Covenant promised the Covenant of Grace by requiring the physical seed of Abraham to obey the demands of the Covenant of Works. In other words, the Abrahamic Covenant is dichotomous in its nature because it contains both an unconditional promise for believers and a condition for the physical offspring of Abraham.

Understanding the dichotomous nature of the Abrahamic Covenant helps us to understand how the physical seed of Abraham, including Christ, was born into a covenantal relationship with God based on works. In contrast, the spiritual seed of Abraham are reborn by faith into a covenantal relationship with God based upon grace.

According to the biblical text, Abraham's true children who inherit the promised blessing are only those who have been supernaturally birthed into the Covenant of Grace by being united to Christ by faith. Therefore, only those who are connected to Christ by faith can rightly be counted as God's true people. This excludes unbelieving Jews, Gentiles, and infants who have not yet come to faith. In both the Old and New Testaments, believers alone are the true people of God!

Serving as an overview of the entire book, Chapter 1 will observe the dichotomous nature of the Abrahamic Covenant so we may better understand its unconditional and conditional elements. Chapters 2-7 will offer biblical support for the dichotomous nature of the Abrahamic Covenant. Finally, Chapter 8 will conclude by emphasizing the importance of maintaining the distinction between the Covenant of Works and the Covenant of Grace and between Abraham's physical and spiritual seeds. Part Two will turn our attention to how the dichotomous nature of the Abrahamic Covenant shapes biblical theology. Here the chapters will flesh out a Baptist view of covenant theology through the different biblical covenants of redemptive history.

1

The Dichotomous Nature of the Abrahamic Covenant

The Abrahamic Covenant is not an administration of the Covenant of Grace. There is no doubt that the promises of justification to be received by faith for both Jews and Gentiles were foreshadowed in the Abrahamic Covenant (Gal. 3:8). There is also no doubt that Abraham's faith in God's promises was accounted to him for righteousness (Gen. 15:6; Rom. 4:22). Furthermore, any of Abraham's descendants who trusted in the coming promised seed were justified by faith alone. By faith they became heirs of the promise inheritance. Because of the fidelity of God, the fulfillment of the Abrahamic promises was certain (Gal. 3:18).

However, this is only one side of the story. Though the Abrahamic Covenant promised eternal blessings, and though the Abrahamic Covenant was unconditional for believers like Abraham, the Abrahamic Covenant was conditional. The condition of the covenant was satisfied by the obedience of Christ—the physical seed of Abraham.

There is no textual or theological evidence indicating that Abraham's physical seed were naturally and automatically born into an unconditional covenantal relationship with God.

Rather, it was quite the opposite. Although Abraham's physical seed were born with the privilege of having access to the knowledge of the gospel, they also were born with a covenantal condition to fulfill—they had to be circumcised. Without their obedience to this covenantal condition, the promises of the covenant, even the gospel itself, would go unfulfilled. The hope of the gospel, and the blessing promised to the nations, was dependent upon the physical seed of Abraham keeping the condition. In short, the Abrahamic Covenant promised the Covenant of Grace by means of the physical seed of Abraham keeping the Covenant of Works.

Oh, how Israel and the rest of the world needed Christ! All of salvation depended upon the coming of this one promised seed. For blessing to be poured out upon the nations, Abraham's seed would have to fulfill the demands and the curses of the law. Thankfully, Christ, the true promised seed of Abraham, did just that in His life and death, as proven by His resurrection.

The Dichotomous Nature of the Abrahamic Covenant

The Abrahamic Covenant is dichotomous in nature in that the Abrahamic Covenant is both unconditional for believers (Abraham's spiritual seed) and conditional for Abraham's physical seed. Understanding the dichotomous nature of the Abrahamic Covenant is not something novel. Historically, the early Baptists of the seventeenth century understood that both the promises of the Covenant of Grace and the conditions of the Covenant of Works were exhibited in the Abrahamic Covenant. Particular Baptists (such as Nehemiah Coxe, Robert Howell, John Spilsbury, Thomas Patient, Henry Lawrence, Philip Cary, and Benjamin Keach) taught that the

Abrahamic Covenant consisted of two distinct parts: the physical and the spiritual.[1]

For instance, Hercules Collins claimed, "We must know the Covenant made with Abraham had two parts."[2] John Spilsbury remarked, "There was in Abraham at that time a spiritual seed and a fleshly seed. Between which seeds God has ever distinguished through all their Generations."[3] Henry Lawrence echoed this understanding of the dual nature of the Abrahamic Covenant when he said, "Here you have a distinction as it were of two Abrahams, a begetting Abraham, and a believing Abraham, and also two seeds, the children of the flesh, that is by carnal generation onely, and the children of the promise."[4] Benjamin Keach stated: "God made a twofold Covenant with Abraham, and that circumcision appertained not to the Covenant of Grace, but to the legal covenant God made with Abraham's natural seed."[5] John Tombes, the seventeenth-century Anglican who opposed infant baptism, came to the same conclusion:

> The Covenant made with Abraham, is not a pure Gospel-covenant, but mixt, which I prove; The Covenant takes its denomination from the promises; but the promises are mixt, some Euangelicall, belonging to those to whom the

---

[1] See Pascal Denault, *The Distinctiveness of Baptist Covenant Theology: A Comparison Between Seventeenth-Century Particular Baptist and Paedobaptist Federalism* (Birmingham, AL: Solid Ground Christian Books, 2013), 117-125. For an interesting account of the Philip Cary and John Flavel debate over the proper subjects of baptism, see Joel Beeke and Mark Jones, *A Puritan Theology: Doctrine for Life* (Grand Rapids: Reformation Heritage Books, 2012), 729-739.

[2] Denault, *The Distinctiveness of Baptist Covenant Theology*, 117.

[3] John Spilsbury, A *Treatise Concerning the Lawful Subject of Baptisme* (repr., Magazine, AR: The Old Faith Baptist Church, 1993), 31.

[4] Cited in Pascal Denault, *The Distinctiveness of Baptist Covenant Theology*, 120-121.

[5] From the title of an unpublished book by Benjamin Keach, The Ax Laid to the Root, or, One Blow More at the Foundation of Infant Baptism, and Church Membership, Part 1 (London: B. Keach, 1693).

Gospel belongeth, some are Domestique, or Civill promises, specially respecting the House of Abraham, and of Israel.⁶

Not only did the seventeenth-century Baptists understand the dual nature of Abraham's covenant, they also understood this dual nature to be the ground of the continuity and discontinuity of the rest of the divine covenants. It was for this reason Nehemiah Coxe stated:

> Abraham is to be considered in a double capacity: he is the father of all the true believers and the father and root of the Israelite nation. God entered into covenant with him for both of these seeds and since they are formally distinguished from one another, their covenant interest must necessarily be different and fall under distinct consideration. The blessings appropriate to either must be conveyed in a way agreeable to their peculiar and respective covenant interest. And these things may not be confounded without a manifest hazard to the most important articles in the Christian religion.⁷

More recently, Stephen Wellum stated that the "Abrahamic Covenant consist of unconditional/unilateral and conditional/bilateral elements and it is not reducible to one of those features alone."⁸

---

⁶ John Tombes, Two Treatises; and an Appendix to them Concerning Infant Baptisme. The Former Treatise being an Exercitation presented to the Chair-man of a Committee of the Assembly of Divines. The latter an Examen of the Sermon of Mr. Stephen Marshall, about Infant-Baptisme, in a letter sent to him (London: 1645).

⁷ Nehemiah Coxe, "A Discourse of the Covenants," in *Covenant Theology: From Adam to Christ*, eds. Ronald D. Miller, James M. Renihan, and Francisco Orozco (Palmdale, CA: Reformed Baptist Academic Press, 2005), 72-73.

⁸ Wellum and Gentry, *Kingdom through Covenant*, 634

A Single Covenant with Two Dimensions

To help us understand why the seventeenth-century Baptists came to such a conclusion, we must turn our attention to the nature of the Abrahamic Covenant.

The Abrahamic Covenant promised three basic things: (1) a land, (2) a kingship, and (3) a people (Gen. 17:6-8). Interestingly, a region of dominion, a king, and a people are the three major elements that constitute a kingdom. Thus, in essence, God promised in the Abrahamic Covenant to establish the Kingdom of God through the seed of Abraham.

The promised kingdom of the Abrahamic Covenant has two dimensions:

A Temporal Dimension	An Eternal Dimension
Type	Antitype
Natural	Supernatural
Bilateral	Unilateral
Conditional	Unconditional

It is important to note that the Abrahamic Covenant is not two covenants, but a single covenant. Like a coin, the Abrahamic Covenant is a single entity with two sides. These two sides, for the most part, coincide with the different emphases within the Old and New Testaments.

In the Old Testament, we see the unfolding and fulfillment of the conditional and temporal side of the Abrahamic Covenant among the physical seed of Abraham. The physical seed of Abraham inherited the physical land of Canaan, and they became a geopolitical nation that was eventually ruled by the royal line of King David. The prosperity of this physical kingdom depended upon national obedience to God.

In the New Testament, we see the unfolding of a spiritual or heavenly kingdom. By faith, Abraham's spiritual seed inherit and secured a place in the heavenly kingdom. King Jesus, at His death and resurrection, began the process of taking dominion and subduing all things to Himself.

Notwithstanding these differences in emphasis, we observe in both the Old and New Testaments the two dimensions of the kingdom of God, one natural and the other supernatural. We need to remember that both dimensions have their roots in the Abrahamic Covenant.

Physical Kingdom	Spiritual Kingdom
Natural	Supernatural
Canaan	Heaven
Physical Seed	Spiritual Seed
The Line of David	King Jesus
Israel	Christ and the Church

The dichotomous nature of the Abrahamic Covenant can be seen in the unfolding of the covenantal history of redemption. After Adam sinned and broke God's law (the Covenant of Works), the curse of the law was poured out justly upon Adam and all his posterity. In Adam, all died. Universal depravity is the proof that mankind has been judged guilty in Adam. Out of this judgment, thankfully, came mercy and the promise of grace. The moment God issued forth judgment upon the world was the moment He also revealed the gospel to the world (Gen. 3:15). In judging the Serpent, the Lord vowed that the seed of the woman (i.e., the coming Messiah) would crush the Serpent's head. Therefore, from the very beginning, we see that grace comes out of judgment and life comes from death. The message is clear: if there is no judgment, there can be no grace.

The Covenantal History of Redemption

This is also true regarding salvation. Salvation is not free. We are justified by works, but the works that justify us are not our own. The high cost of our salvation was paid by Christ's own blood. The law could not be removed until it was fulfilled in both its conditions and penalties. For God to be just and the justifier of the ungodly, the legal demands of the law had to be satisfied (Rom. 3:21-26). A life of perfect obedience was needed. Therefore, salvation is free for the sinner who believes but not for the Savior. Christ merited perfect righteousness by keeping the conditions of the law of God. In addition, He paid for His people's sins by taking on the curses of the law while upon the cross (Gal. 3:13).

Thus, we see the Covenant of Grace could not have been established without the full satisfaction and fulfillment of the Covenant of Works. In this the Covenant of Grace is the fulfillment of the Covenant of Works. In other words, if there was not the Covenant of Works, there could not have been the Covenant of Grace.

After sin entered the historical narrative, it was not possible for the Covenant of Works and the conditions of the law to fade away. Rather, the demands of the law had to remain in force. Just because the unrighteous cannot keep the Covenant of Works does not mean the Covenant of Works ceases to demand righteousness for all those born under the legal headship of Adam.

Moreover, if there had been no Covenant of Works to fulfill, then there could not have been a Covenant of Grace to reveal. Therefore, until the cross of Calvary, the legal demands of the Covenant of Works had to be a major component in the overall history of redemption.

What is a covenant? Basically, a divine covenant consists of the legal and binding terms of a relationship with God.[9] Since God is God, He sets the terms of the relationship. Because God is morally perfect, the terms of the relationship can be nothing other than perfect righteousness. Without righteousness, no one can see God. The consequence of sin is always separation from God. These terms never change. Therefore, reconciliation with God requires the establishment of perfect righteousness.

Therefore, the essence of the Covenant of Works is God's moral law. God's law functions as a covenant as it cannot help but demand perfect obedience and promises life for those who obey and threaten death for those who disobey. Because God is just, God does not enter relationships without demanding perfect righteousness. For this reason, God's relationship with man is never outside of a covenant.

The Covenant of Works and the Covenant of Grace both contain the legal terms for a relationship with God. The Covenant of Works contains the terms of God's relationship with those outside of Christ, thus condemning its membership. The Covenant of Grace contains the terms of the relationship upon those in Christ, thus forgiving its membership. The law exists in both the Covenant of Works and the Covenant of Grace. However, the law is yet to be fulfilled for those in the Covenant of Works, while the law has

---

[9] Walter Chantry defines a covenant as "a sovereignly given arrangement by which man may be blessed" (*The Covenants of Works and of Grace*, 91). Michael Horton defines a covenant as "a relationship of 'oaths and bonds' [that] involves mutual, though not necessarily equal, commitments" (*God of Promise*, 10). O. Palmer Robertson likewise stated, "This closeness of relationship between oath and covenant emphasizes that a covenant in its essence is a bond. By the covenant, persons become committed to one another" (*The Christ of the Covenants*, 7). Peter Gentry says, "At the heart of covenant, then, is a relationship between parties characterized by faithfulness and loyalty in love (*Kingdom through Covenant*, 141).

already been fulfilled in Christ for those in the Covenant of Grace. As Walter Chantry observed:

> You live under either the Covenant of Works or the Covenant of Grace. There are none other but these two... Under the Covenant of Grace, the identical demand must be met. No lesser obedience will be accepted. Under the Covenant of Works the curse pronounced for sin is death. Man sinned and death must be the result. Under the Covenant of Grace a Mediator must fulfill perfect righteousness for men who cannot provide it of themselves. The Mediator will also die under the curse of the Covenant of Works in the place of sinners. The heel of the Seed of the woman is bruised, "Christ hath redeemed us from the curse of the law, being made a curse for us..." (Gal 3:13). He did this not by abolishing law or by invalidating the Covenant of Works, but by "being made a curse for us." He met all the demands of the Covenant of Works. He fulfilled all its terms.[10]

Chantry also notes,

> The Lord required perfect and universal righteousness in both. The definition of righteousness is unchanged from the Covenant of Works to the Covenant of Grace. But in another sense everything is at opposite poles. In the Covenant of Works man must earn by his doing. In the Covenant of Grace, man must receive the free gift from a Mediator by believing.[11]

So then, there is no grace without judgment. The overall history of redemption plays out these two covenants, one of works and one of grace, in which history finds its ultimate

---

[10] Chantry, *The Covenants of Works and Grace*, 103.
[11] Chantry, *The Covenants of Works and Grace*, 97-98.

fulfillment in the cross of Calvary, where justice and mercy embrace.

The Davidic Covenant

Our effort to understand the dichotomous nature of the Abrahamic Covenant may be helped by observing a similar dichotomy in the Davidic Covenant. Was the Davidic Covenant rooted in the Covenant of Works or in the Covenant of Grace? Was the promise to David conditional or unconditional? The answer depends upon who is asked. If we asked King David, he would respond by saying that the promise of an eternal kingship was unconditional. Yet if we asked any of David's children, they would have to answer by saying that they had been given a legal condition to obey.

These unconditional and conditional dimensions of the Davidic Covenant are clearly seen in Psalm 132:11-12: "The LORD swore [unconditionally] to David a sure oath from which he will not turn back: 'One of the sons of your body I will set on your throne. If your sons [conditionally] keep my covenant and my testimonies that I shall teach them, their sons also forever shall sit on your throne.'"[12] David understood that although God would be faithful in fulfilling His promise to him, his royal line would be obligated to obey the Mosaic Law to remain upon the throne. For this reason, David sternly warned his son, Solomon, to obey God:

> When David's time to die drew near, he commanded Solomon his son, saying, "I am about to go the way of all the earth. Be strong, and show yourself a man, and keep the charge of the LORD your God, walking in his ways and keeping his statutes, his commandments, his rules, and his testimonies, as it is written in the Law of Moses, that you

---

[12] Words in brackets are mine.

may prosper in all that you do and wherever you turn, that the LORD may establish his word that he spoke concerning me, saying, 'If your sons pay close attention to their way, to walk before me in faithfulness with all their heart and with all their soul, you shall not lack a man on the throne of Israel' (1 Kings 2:1-4).

Years later Jeremiah reminded the sons of David that they were under the Covenant of Works:

> Thus says the LORD: "Go down to the house of the king of Judah and speak there this word, and say, 'Hear the word of the LORD, O king of Judah, who sits on the throne of David, you, and your servants, and your people who enter these gates. Thus says the LORD: Do justice and righteousness, and deliver from the hand of the oppressor him who has been robbed. And do no wrong or violence to the resident alien, the fatherless, and the widow, nor shed innocent blood in this place. For if you will indeed obey this word, then there shall enter the gates of this house kings who sit on the throne of David, riding in chariots and on horses, they and their servants and their people. But if you will not obey these words, I swear by myself, declares the LORD, that this house shall become a desolation (Jer. 22:1-5).

Admittedly, it would have been pointless for God to give a promise to David that was dependent upon David's children keeping the law if it were not for the fact that the promise was speaking of Christ Jesus and His future obedience. Solomon succeeded David, but it was not Solomon whom God ultimately had in mind when He established the Davidic Covenant. Rather, it was Jesus Christ. For Christ was not only a descendant of David, but He was also the only descendant of David that perfectly kept the law, as evidenced by His resurrection from the dead.

Peter picked up this theme in his famous sermon on the day of Pentecost. After pointing out that David was convinced that one of his descendants would sit upon his throne forever, Peter proclaimed that this promise was fulfilled at the resurrection of Christ from the dead:

> Brothers, I may say to you with confidence about the patriarch David that he both died and was buried, and his tomb is with us to this day. Being therefore a prophet, and knowing that God had sworn with an oath to him that he would set one of his descendants on his throne, he foresaw and spoke about the resurrection of the Christ, that he was not abandoned to Hades, nor did his flesh see corruption. This Jesus God raised up, and of that we all are witnesses. Being therefore exalted at the right hand of God, and having received from the Father the promise of the Holy Spirit, he has poured out this that you yourselves are seeing and hearing. For David did not ascend into the heavens, but he himself says, "The Lord said to my Lord, 'Sit at my right hand, until I make your enemies your footstool.'" Let all the house of Israel therefore know for certain that God has made him both Lord and Christ, this Jesus whom you crucified (Acts 2:29-36).

Christ, the son of David, is qualified to sit upon an everlasting throne because He was declared righteous in His resurrection. Without this legal righteousness, Christ would have remained in the grave, and the establishment of the kingdom, promised to Abraham and David, would not have been accomplished.

Many other parallels could be pointed out between the Abrahamic and Davidic Covenants, such as the types and antitypes, temporal and eternal elements, and the natural and supernatural dimensions of each. Nevertheless, this understanding of the unconditional and conditional sides of the Davidic Covenant is sufficient to help us better understand the dichotomous nature of the Abrahamic Covenant.

Conclusion

The objective of Part 1 of this book is to prove the Abrahamic Covenant was a dichotomous covenant. A dichotomous covenant is a single covenant with two separate dimensions: spiritual and physical, eternal and temporal, and unconditional and conditional. The important thing to note is that Abraham's physical seed belonged to the conditional side of the Abrahamic Covenant, while Abraham's spiritual seed belong to the unconditional side of the Abrahamic Covenant.

Conditional	Unconditional
Physical Seed	Spiritual Seed

Understanding the dual nature of the Abrahamic Covenant is vital in understanding the continuity and discontinuity between the divine covenants. Ultimately, it helps us to answer two questions: Who are the true people of God? What is the true nature of the kingdom of God? In the next few chapters, we will attempt to prove the dichotomous nature of the Abrahamic Covenant by observing the wording, the fulfillment, the New Testament interpretation, and the two memberships of the Abrahamic Covenant.

2

The Wording of the Abrahamic Covenant

Presbyterian covenantalism states that the Abrahamic, Mosaic, and New Covenants are administrations of the Covenant of Grace.[1] For this reason they say the New Covenant is essentially the same as the Old Covenant. Baptist covenantalism, on the other hand, states that the Abrahamic and Mosaic Covenants were republications of the Covenant of Works, while the New Covenant is the Covenant of Grace. The Old and New Covenants are not essentially the same.

Baptist covenantalism, however, states that both the Mosaic and New Covenants were born out of the conditional and unconditional dimensions of the Abrahamic Covenant, respectively. The Mosaic Covenant flows out of the conditions the Abrahamic Covenant placed on Abraham's physical descendants, while the New Covenant flows out of the gospel promised to Abraham.

How can a single covenant be unconditional and conditional at the same time? At first glance, this seems

---

[1] See O. Palmer Robertson, *The Christ of the Covenants* (Phillipsburg, NJ: P&R, 1980), 28-31.

contradictory. The only way for this to be true (and not self-refuting) is for the conditions of the Abrahamic Covenant to belong to Abraham's physical seed, while the unconditional promises belong to Abraham's spiritual seed.

The objective of the next few chapters is to prove, from the Scriptures, that the Abrahamic Covenant was both unconditional and conditional. We will seek to prove this assertion by (1) the wording of the Abrahamic Covenant, (2) the actual fulfillment of the Abrahamic Covenant, (3) and the teaching of the New Testament.

The Wording of the Abrahamic Covenant

The first place to turn in understanding the nature and terms of the Abrahamic Covenant is to the canonical text in which the covenant was originally recorded. The promises and terms of the covenant are found in Genesis 17:6-14. In this passage, we uncover the basic unconditional and conditional dimensions of the Abrahamic Covenant.

Unconditional Promises

In verses 6-8, we notice the certainty and unconditional nature of these promises:

> *I will* make you exceedingly fruitful, and *I will* make you into nations, and kings shall come from you. And *I will* establish my covenant between me and you and your offspring after you throughout their generations for an everlasting covenant, to be God to you and to your offspring after you. And *I will* give to you and to your offspring after you the land of your sojournings, all the land of Canaan, for an everlasting possession, and *I will* be their God.[2]

---

[2] Emphasis is mine.

The certainty of these promises is seen in the fact that it is God Himself who has made them. The words "I will" are consistently repeated in these verses, and they are powerful words when coming from a God who cannot lie. Abraham trusted God, for he knew the foundation of the promises was based upon the fidelity of God. In this way, the promises were certain and unconditional to the one who received them by faith.

Conditional Promises

The language in the next few verses shifts away from certain fulfillment to the real possibility of some of Abraham's physical seed being "cut off" and separated from the people of God. In verses 9-14, we observe the conditional side of the covenant:

> And God said to Abraham, "As for you, *you shall* keep my covenant, you and your offspring after you throughout their generations. This is my covenant, which *you shall* keep, between me and you and your offspring after you: Every male among *you shall* be circumcised. [...] Any uncircumcised male who is not circumcised in the flesh of his foreskin shall be cut off from his people; he has broken my covenant" (Gen. 17:9-10, 14).[3]

The language turns from "I will," to "you shall." The responsible party has shifted from God to Abraham and to his physical seed.

Even more telling is that this covenant is said to be breakable. Those who were not circumcised have "broken" the covenant. Even Moses almost died in the wilderness

---

[3] Emphasis is mine.

because he neglected his duty to circumcise his children (Ex. 4:24-26).

In this, we see all the ingredients of a Covenant of Works: (1) a condition—circumcision, (2) covenant breakers—the uncircumcised, and (3) sanctions—being either united or "cut off" from God and His people.

The conditional nature of the promise blessing of the Abrahamic Covenant would seem merely hypothetical and pointless if it were not for the fact that there was one seed of Abraham who did obey and fulfill the condition of the covenant. Since the promised seed was speaking of Christ, then both the promise and condition of the Abrahamic Covenant were certain to be fulfilled.

> Now the promises were made to Abraham and to his offspring. It does not say, 'And to offsprings,' referring to many, but referring to one, 'And to your offspring,' who is Christ" (Gal. 3:16).

In other words, God did not promise Abraham that every physical descendant of his (i.e., Ishmael, Esau, and all his children from his second wife - Keturah) would be counted among the children of promise. Rather, the promised seed was in reference to one child in particular - Jesus Christ. Other than Jesus Christ, the rest of Abraham's physical descendants were not given any unconditional guarantee that they would not be "cut off" from the covenant. Paul made this clear when he said, "not all who are descended from Israel belong to Israel, and not all are children of Abraham because they are his offspring (Rom. 9:6b-7a).

Nevertheless, every physical descendant of Abraham, even Christ, was placed under the legal condition of obedience. However, as we shall see, Christ was the only physical seed of Abraham who kept the covenant. Thus, only Christ and those who are united to Christ by faith are the fulfillment of the promised seed.

The Significance of Circumcision

The condition of the Abrahamic Covenant was circumcision, yet this condition implied more than the outward cutting of the flesh. For example, the single command given to Adam and Eve not to eat of the forbidden fruit included full obedience of the moral law of God.[4] The law demands that we love God with all our heart, soul, and mind, and that we love our neighbor as ourselves (Matt. 22:37-40). By one act of disobedience, Adam broke the entire law (James 2:10). Adam's single act of rebellion displayed a fundamental lack of love for God and a lack of love for his neighbor.

In the same way, keeping the condition of circumcision implied more than one simple act of outward obedience. Rather, it symbolized full obedience of the law from the heart (Deut. 30:6). This was the assessment of the Lord Jesus: "Moses gave you circumcision (not that it is from Moses, but from the fathers), and you circumcise a man on the Sabbath. ...on the Sabbath a man receives circumcision, so that the law

---

[4] Samuel Jones stated: "Adam, in eating the forbidden fruit, in a manner broke every precept of the moral law; for, he was guilty of setting up another God, of trampling on the authority of the true God, and profaning his holy name; when, he gave him the lie, disbelieved his word, disobeyed his command, and transferred all the honour of faith, worship, obedience, and hope, to another. He dishonored his parent in the highest manner. He was guilty of murder in murdering himself and posterity, soul and body. He was guilty of theft and robbery, in robbing God of his glory, himself and posterity of innocence and happiness. While to receive a false witness, and act upon it, was no better than to bear false witness. And, finally, he coveted the goods and property of another; and not only coveted, but took possession of, and devoured at once. Nor would it be difficult to show that this one sin involved in it, infidelity, pride, ingratitude, contempt, folly, cruelty, and those other affections and aggravations of sin (*The Doctrine of the Covenants: A Sermon Preached at Pennepeck in Pennsylvania,* Sep. 14, 1783. Philadelphia: F. Bailey, 1783. 15).

of Moses may not be broken." (Jn. 7:22-23). Moreover, the apostle Paul understood that circumcision could not be disjoined from the law of God: "I testify again to every man who accepts circumcision that he is obligated to keep the whole law" (Gal. 5:3). "For circumcision indeed is of value if you obey the law, but if you break the law, your circumcision becomes uncircumcision" (Rom. 2:25).

This connection between circumcision and perfect obedience is not merely a New Testament understanding of circumcision, for even the Old Testament explained that the blessings of the Abrahamic Covenant were contingent upon the righteousness of the physical seed of Abraham:

> The LORD said, "Shall I hide from Abraham what I am about to do, seeing that Abraham shall surely become a great and mighty nation, and all the nations of the earth shall be blessed in him? For I have chosen him, that he may command his children and his household after him to keep the way of the LORD *by doing righteousness and justice, so that the LORD may bring to Abraham what he has promised him*" (Gen. 18:17-19).[5]

In other words, for the nations of the world to be blessed, the seed of Abraham was required not only to be circumcised, but also to be righteous.

Covenantal Presbyterians are correct, therefore, when they press the importance of the spiritual and inward significance of circumcision. Circumcision meant more than an outward act of obedience; it also signified the cutting away of the old fleshly nature and loving God from a renewed heart (Col. 2:11-12). For instance, G. K. Beale stated, "Circumcision represented...the 'cutting off of the flesh' to designate that the sinful flesh around the heart was cut off, signifying the regeneration

---

[5] Emphasis is mine.

of the heart and the setting apart of a person to the Lord."[6] In essence, this means that outward circumcision spoke of the need for the Jews to have a circumcised heart.

The problem, however, was that circumcision of the flesh did not promise, produce, or secure a circumcised heart. There was no saving efficacy in fleshly circumcision. In other words, fleshly circumcision demanded love for God but was unable to produce a love for God. This is why Moses told the unbelieving children of Abraham to circumcise the foreskins of their heart (Deut. 10:16). Moses understood that outward circumcision alone was inadequate in setting apart a people for God.

Jeremiah also understood this (Jer. 4:4). Jeremiah warned the Jews that those who did not circumcise their hearts would be "cut off" from God: "Behold, the days are coming, declares the LORD, when I will punish all those who are circumcised merely in the flesh" (Jer. 9:25).

The Apostle Paul confirmed this Old Testament teaching by explaining the reason why outward circumcision alone was insufficient in producing the children of God: "For no one is a Jew who is merely one outwardly, nor is circumcision outward and physical. But a Jew is one inwardly, and circumcision is a matter of the heart, by the Spirit, not by the letter. His praise is not from man but from God" (Rom. 2:28-29). In short, being placed under the law of circumcision did not produce the ability to obey the law that was signified by circumcision.

Moreover, the impossibility of circumcising one's own heart did not nullify the responsibility for the Jews to love God with all their heart, mind, and soul. Moral inability does not

---

[6] G. K. Beale, *A New Testament Biblical Theology: The Unfolding of the Old Testament in the New* (Grand Rapids: Baker, 2011), 812-813.

render God's commands hypothetical; the condition is binding even if it is impossible to fulfil. It is impossible to have a relationship with God without holiness (Heb. 12:14).

Therefore, as we have seen, circumcision explained that perfect righteousness was needed to have a relationship with God. For instance, because Abraham was circumcised after he believed, his circumcision was the "seal of the righteousness that he had by faith while he was still uncircumcised" (Rom. 4:11).

In other words, *credo-circumcision* signified the blessings of the law for those who have been given the imputed righteousness of Christ by faith. Yet for those who received circumcision without faith, their circumcision signified the righteousness that was still required of them. In other words, *paedo-circumcision* signified the curses of the law that remained upon those without faith. As G. K. Beale acknowledges, circumcision also "represented being 'cut off' from the Lord."[7] Thus, circumcision signified the blessing and curses of the law.

There is good news, however. Even though circumcision placed the physical children of Abraham under unbearable demands in which they could not satisfy, they still had hope of salvation. The same covenant that demanded obedience also promised the gospel. By believing the unconditional promise that was given to Abraham, Abraham's physical children could legally be declared righteous. Like Abraham, they could be declared righteous apart from outward circumcision and apart from obedience to the law (Rom. 4:9-12). Abraham's physical seed could become Abraham's spiritual seed—and this not by works but by faith. By the Holy Spirit's gift of faith, their outward circumcision could be transformed into inner

---

[7] Beale, *A New Testament Biblical Theology*, 812-813.

circumcision. By faith, the law that was externally engraved upon their flesh could be internally written upon their hearts.

Though Abraham's physical seed were born under the Covenant of Works, they were blessed with access to the gospel. By faith, apart from circumcision, the Jews could be declared righteous in Christ and receive the imputed reality of what was outwardly commanded of them by circumcision (Rom. 3).

However, it is important to note that even though salvation in the Old Testament was by grace through faith, there remained the necessity for Abraham's physical seed (Christ Jesus) to keep the law. As it is written, salvation would come from the Jews (Jn. 4:22). All hope for salvation in the Old Testament would be lost if this did not occur. To bring salvation and blessings to the nations, including the nation of Israel, the law had to be satisfied. The circumcision of the Abrahamic Covenant demanded that the heirs of the promises be holy and set apart before God. There was no way around this. Although the Abrahamic Covenant promised the gospel, it also placed all of Abraham's physical seed under the Covenant of Works.

Thankfully, the seed of Abraham did come and fulfill the righteous demands of the law. "For I tell you that Christ became a servant to the circumcised to show God's truthfulness, in order to confirm the promises given to the patriarchs, and in order that the Gentiles might glorify God for his mercy" (Rom. 15:8-9a). This is why Genesis 18:19 says the physical seed of Abraham had to "keep the way of the LORD by doing righteousness and justice, so that the LORD may bring to Abraham what he has promised him."

By this means, the tension between a conditional and unconditional covenant is safely resolved, as Stephen Wellum explained:

> The tension, then, created in the relationship is that God guarantees the covenant promises and yet, he also requires an obedient son in the covenant relationship. That demand, however, is only met, finally and fully, in the true seed of Abraham, our Lord Jesus Christ.[8]

The Abrahamic Covenant is like a rich man promising a poor man a million dollars if the poor man's son earned the million dollars. Except in this case, the promise ensured that the poor man's son would indeed earn the million dollars. In the same way, God promised Abraham that His son (Jesus) would fulfill the law and bring blessings to the nations of the world. Abraham believed the promise, and it was counted to him as righteousness.

Conclusion

The wording of the terms of the Abrahamic Covenant reveals its dichotomous nature. The Abrahamic Covenant promised the Covenant of Grace by reminding the physical seed of Abraham that they were born under the condition of the Covenant of Works. The Abrahamic Covenant promised that the New Covenant would establish grace for the spiritual seed of Abraham because the physical seed of Abraham would fulfill the law of the Old Covenant. As we shall see, that promised physical seed was Christ Jesus. Thus, to describe the Abrahamic Covenant as an administration of the Covenant of Grace is to rush over or ignore the condition, breakability, and curse of the Abrahamic Covenant.

---

[8] Gentry and Wellum, *Kingdom through Covenant* (Wheaton, IL: Crossway, 1012).

3

Abraham's Two Seeds

Not only does the wording of the Abrahamic Covenant reveal its dichotomous nature; the actual working out and fulfillment of the covenant in redemptive history verifies its two-sided (conditional and unconditional) character. The promise of a kingdom was slowly and progressively fulfilled in the Old Testament in a conditional, typological, and temporal fashion. In the New Testament, the promised kingdom is being progressively established in an unconditional, antitypical, and eternal fashion. The physical descendants of Abraham were established into a geopolitical nation which eventually crumbled because of their disobedience. Abraham's spiritual seed, on the other hand, have been born again into a spiritual kingdom which is eternal because of the imputed righteousness of its citizenship.

However, these two kingdoms (temporal and eternal) do not represent two distinct and separate promises or plans of God. Rather, these two kingdoms work together to fulfill God's overall covenantal plan of redemption, for they are both born out of the same Abrahamic Covenant. As we shall see, the temporal kingdom foreshadowed, served, and eventually assisted in the establishment of the eternal kingdom. Thus, the eternal kingdom does not replace the temporal kingdom, but rather fulfills it.

Abraham's Two Sons

The two-pronged fulfillment of the Abrahamic Covenant is immediately seen in the two sons of Abraham: Ishmael and Isaac. Ishmael was born of the flesh while Isaac was born of the promise. These two children represent the two types of seeds (physical and spiritual) of Abraham (Gal. 4:21-31). According to the Apostle Paul, Ishmael represents the physical descendants of Abraham that occupy the storyline of the Old Testament, while Isaac represents the spiritual children of Abraham that occupy the storyline of the New Testament.

- Ishmael = The Natural Seed of Abraham
- Isaac = The Supernatural Seed of Abraham

The physical seed are the natural children of Abraham; the spiritual seed are the supernatural children of Abraham. The physical seed were circumcised in the flesh; the spiritual seed have been circumcised in heart. The physical seed inherited an earthly land for a moment of time; the spiritual seed are heirs to a heavenly city whose builder and maker is God. The physical seed was born into a geopolitical nation; the spiritual seed have been reborn into the heavenly kingdom of God.

The differences between the physical and spiritual seeds of Abraham manifest the dichotomous fulfillment of the Abrahamic Covenant. In chapter 4, we will discover how the physical seed inherited the Mosaic Covenant that was based on works; and in Chapter 5, we will explore how the spiritual seed have inherited the New Covenant that is based on grace.

The Natural Seed and the Mosaic Covenant

To understand the role of Abraham's natural offspring, we must keep in mind that the condition of the Abrahamic Covenant could not have been removed until it was fulfilled. Therefore, every physical descendant of Abraham, even Christ, was born under its legal and binding obligation. As explained in the previous chapter, the condition was obedience, and obedience was symbolized by circumcision. Circumcision was a boundary marker that separated Abraham's seed from the rest of the world and distinguished the children of Abraham as the family through which the Messiah would come. Those who were not circumcised were cut off and separated from God and His people.

Yet, as we have seen, circumcision called for more than just the outward cutting of the flesh. It demanded circumcision of the heart. A circumcised heart is the sign of the child of God, for inward holiness, not mere outward conformity, has always been the true identifying mark of God's people.

The problem, however, with all of Abraham's physical children (besides Christ) was that they were born with uncircumcised hearts. Due to their inward depravity, they were born already spiritually "cut off" from God. Being physically and outwardly circumcised children of Abraham did not change their legal standing before God (Rom. 2:6-29). Abraham's children may have been born privileged, having access to the gospel, but they were also born depraved. Because of Adam's sin nature, which passed to them through Abraham, the children of Abraham were born not into a state of grace but into a state of condemnation and under the wrath of God (Rom. 3:9).

Thankfully, hope for salvation remained for the Israelites. As with Abraham and the rest of the believing remnant in the

Old Testament, Abraham's physical seed could turn from trusting in their own righteousness by looking to and trusting in the coming Messiah. They could forsake all confidence in the flesh (which would include not trusting in their status as outwardly circumcised children of Abraham) and place their full confidence in the promised seed who would keep the condition of the covenant on their behalf. Like Abraham, Old Testament Jews could certainly be saved, but it had to be by faith, not simply because they were Jewish.

To help point Abraham's physical seed to the coming Messiah, God established the Mosaic Covenant with the house of Israel. The Mosaic Covenant was established not with Abraham, Isaac, and Jacob, but with the whole congregation of Israel. It was given to Israel to manifest their innate sinfulness (Rom. 3:20). The law was given, not to save the children of Israel, but to condemn them. That is, God gave them the law to help them see more clearly that they were already unrighteous and guilty before God under the Covenant of Works established with Adam—their federal head (Rom. 3:19).

The law was also designed to be a schoolmaster to lead Israel to Christ (Gal. 3:21-25). The law was not given to nullify faith in the promise but to point Abraham's children away from faith in themselves (Gal. 3:22). Being circumcised children of Abraham was of no value to the Jews unless they could keep the whole law (Rom. 2:25). Therefore, the Law of Moses given to them was to call them to repentance, and the promise given to Abraham was given to call them to believe the gospel. "But the Scripture imprisoned everything under sin, so that the promise by faith in Jesus Christ might be given to those who believe" (Gal. 3:22).

In some ways, therefore, the Mosaic Covenant was unlike the Abrahamic Covenant. Yet in other ways, the Mosaic Covenant was nothing more than the outworking of the Covenant of Works that had underpinned the conditional requirements of the Abrahamic Covenant (Gen. 17:9-14).

The Discontinuity between the Abrahamic and Mosaic Covenants

As the outworking of the conditional side of the Abrahamic Covenant, the Mosaic Covenant stood in direct contrast to the unconditional side of the Abrahamic Covenant. That is, unlike the Abrahamic Covenant, the Mosaic Covenant contained no unconditional promises (Gal. 3:16-18). For this reason, Moses made sure the Israelites understood the difference between law and promise when he distinguished the Mosaic Covenant from the Abrahamic Covenant:

> And Moses summoned all Israel and said to them, "Hear, O Israel, the statutes and the rules that I speak in your hearing today, and you shall learn them and be careful to do them. The LORD our God made a covenant with us in Horeb. Not with our fathers did the LORD make this covenant, but with us, who are all of us here alive today (Deut. 5:1-4).

In distinguishing the Israelite children from the Fathers (Abraham, Isaac, and Jacob), Moses highlighted the discontinuity between the Abrahamic and Mosaic Covenants. Abraham, Isaac, and Jacob were promised that the Messiah would be one of their personal descendants. Yet, after Israel was divided into twelve tribes, the average Israelite could not assume that he might be the father of the Messiah. What could be said of Abraham, Isaac, and Jacob—"in your seed all the nations of the earth shall be blessed"—could not be said for the children of Dan, Reuben, or the majority of the other

Israelites. The unconditional promise was established with the Fathers, not with every physical child of Abraham.

The Mosaic Covenant was different from the Abrahamic Covenant in that the Mosaic Covenant was established, not just with the direct genealogical line of Christ, but with every Israelite without exception. The Mosaic Covenant was a national covenant. The Fathers were given a promise, while the nation of Israel was given the law.

Moreover, the promise given to Abraham was not to be confused with the law given by Moses. The law and the gospel are not the same. The Abrahamic Covenant promised the Covenant of Grace, but as we shall see, the essence of the Mosaic Covenant was a republication of the Covenant of Works that was previously established with Adam.

The Continuity between the Abrahamic and Mosaic Covenants

To understand the continuity between the Abrahamic and Mosaic Covenants, we must understand the differences between God's moral law and positive laws.

God's moral law, in which all divine covenants are rooted, is based on the very nature of God. God's moral law reflects God's own moral character. God did not look to a moral code outside Himself, for He is the foundation of morality. More precisely, because the law is legal and relational by its very nature, God's law reflects the inner Trinitarian relationship between the Father, Son, and Holy Spirit. The relationship between the Father, Son, and Spirit is rooted in love. Because God's moral law, summarized in the ten commandments, is rooted in God's love, it cannot be altered, changed, or abrogated. Moreover, every covenant God has established with man had to be based on this perfect and eternal standard.

Positive laws, on the other hand, are the various commands of God that are unique to a particular covenant. Positive laws are rooted in God's moral law. For instance, the command not to eat the fruit of the Tree of the Knowledge of Good and Evil in the Adamic Covenant, and the command to be circumcised in the Abrahamic Covenant, and the command not to eat pork in the Mosaic Covenant are based on God's moral law. Positive laws do not necessarily transcend the particular covenant in which they were issued. Since we are no longer under the Adamic Covenant, we don't have any trees to stay away from. Yet, as long as any particular covenant stood, to transgress any positive law was to transgress the moral law. For instance, when Adam and Eve eat the forbidden fruit, they transgress the moral law that transcends every covenantal arrangement.

With the distinction between moral and positive law, we can better see the unity (and discontinuity) between the Adamic, Abrahamic, and Mosaic Covenants. This is because the unity between the Abrahamic and Mosaic Covenant is rooted in the unchanging and eternal moral law that undergirds all the covenants of God. While the disunity, in part, is found in the different positive laws that are unique to the Adamic, Abrahamic, and Mosaic Covenants.

The essence of the Adamic Covenant is the moral law of God. Though the positive law of not eating the forbidden fruit is no longer applicable, the moral law behind that probation remains unchanged. Just because God's moral law was broken and its curses executed upon Adam and his descendants, does not mean that its demands for perfect righteousness have been repelled or abrogated. Just because the fallen seed of Adam cannot keep the moral law does not mean they are not accountable to God's moral law. In this sense, the Covenant of Works undergirded the Adamic Covenant remains binding on humanity.

Like the Adamic Covenant, the essence of the Abrahamic Covenant is also rooted in God's moral law. The positive law that was unique to this covenant (and reissued in the Mosaic Covenant) is found in the command to be circumcised. Yet, as we have seen, circumcision is also rooted in God's moral law. Again, God never issues any positive laws that are not based on His own righteous moral standard. The command to be circumcised demanded full obedience to the moral law. In this sense, the Abrahamic Covenant reminded Abraham and his seed that they remain under the Covenant of Works that was first issued with Adam—their federal head.

In addition, the Mosaic Covenant is also rooted in God's moral law. For instance, the heart of the Mosaic Covenant is the ten commandments, which can be reduced to loving God with all your heart and loving your neighbor as yourself. Though the Mosaic Covenant included all kinds of new positive laws (such as not eating pork, etc.), the heart of the Mosaic Covenant remained the same as the Adamic and Abrahamic Covenants of works. The Mosaic Covenant is not the same covenant as the Abrahamic or the Adamic Covenants (as they have different participants and different positive laws), they all are expressions or administrations of the Covenant of Works—the eternal covenant that cannot stop its demands and threats until it is fully satisfied (in Christ).

The discontinuity between the promise of the Abrahamic Covenant and the law of the Mosaic Covenant leads to the continuity between these two covenants. For instance, the promise of the Abrahamic Covenant was that the physical seed of Abraham would fulfill the law of the Mosaic Covenant and thus bring blessings to the nations. To understand the nature of the continuity between the Abrahamic and the Mosaic Covenants, we must remember that the oath that was established with Abraham, and personally reaffirmed with Isaac and Jacob, guaranteed that the coming Messiah would be one of their direct descendants (Gen. 26:2- 5; 28:13-15). We must also keep in mind that, though the promise was given to the Fathers, the condition was given to their children. In other words, the unconditional promise that God gave to Abraham, Isaac, and Jacob would not come to fruition unless their seed fulfilled the condition of the covenant.

The condition of the Abrahamic Covenant was circumcision, but the full implications of circumcision remained murky until God gave the physical seed of Abraham a clearer expression of the moral law at Mount Sinai (the ten commandments). Importantly, the Mosaic Covenant did not replace the condition placed upon the physical seed of Abraham in Genesis 17. It merely gave greater clarity to what was already required by circumcision. In other words, the Mosaic Covenant grew out of and codified the conditional side of the Abrahamic Covenant. There are at least five theological reasons why the law did not and could not replace what was already demanded by circumcision.

First, the Mosaic Covenant was established with the physical children of Abraham—the same group of people who were placed under the conditions of the Abrahamic Covenant. If the Abrahamic Covenant had been purely a covenant of grace for the physical seed of Abraham, then it would have been unjust for God to place that same group of people under the Mosaic Covenant of Works. Therefore, the only way the Covenant of Works (republished in the Mosaic Covenant) could have been established with the physical seed of Abraham was for the physical seed of Abraham to have already been obligated to obey the moral law of God in the Abrahamic Covenant.

Second, the covenantal blessings were conditional from the beginning of the Abrahamic Covenant, and they continued to be so under the Mosaic Covenant.

> *Thou shalt* therefore keep the commandments, and the statutes, and the judgments, which I command thee this day, *to do them.* Wherefore it shall come to pass, *if ye hearken* to these judgments, and keep, and *do them*, that the LORD thy God shall keep unto thee the covenant and the mercy which he sware unto thy fathers (Deut. 7:11-12, KJV).[1]

The Promised Land, the eternal kingship, and the establishment of the people of God all were predicated on the fulfillment of the moral law that was at the heart of the Mosaic Covenant. "Now therefore, if you will indeed obey my voice and keep my covenant, you shall be my treasured possession among all peoples, for all the earth is mine; and you shall be to me a kingdom of priests and a holy nation" (Ex. 19:5-6).

Thus, the kingdom promised in the Abrahamic Covenant remained conditional under the Mosaic Covenant. Without the fulfillment of the Mosaic Covenant, the covenant promises to Abraham would go unfulfilled.

Third, obedience to the moral law of God was already the condition of the Abrahamic Covenant. About 400 years prior to the establishment of the Mosaic Covenant, the Lord explained that the blessings promised to Abraham were predicated upon the obedience of the physical seed of Abraham:

> The LORD said, "Shall I hide from Abraham what I am about to do, seeing that Abraham shall surely become a

---

[1] Emphasis is mine.

great and mighty nation, and all the nations of the earth shall be blessed in him? For I have chosen him, that he may command his children and his household after him to keep the way of the LORD by doing righteousness and justice, so that the LORD may bring to Abraham what he has promised him" (Gen. 18:17-19).

Since the conditions listed in Exodus 19 are the same as the conditions that we read of in Genesis 18, it is evident that the Mosaic Covenant did not alter the terms of the blessings of the Abrahamic Covenant. Once the covenant was ratified with the physical seed of Abraham in Genesis 17, the terms and conditions of that covenant could not have been changed four centuries later. Any alteration to the terms placed upon the physical seed of Abraham would have been unjust (Gal. 3:15).

Fourth, the New Testament teaches that the condition of the Mosaic Covenant was the same as the condition of the Abrahamic Covenant. "Moses gave you circumcision (not that it is from Moses, but from the fathers), and you circumcise a man...so that the law of Moses may not be broken..." (Jn. 7:22-23). "For circumcision indeed is of value if you obey the law, but if you break the law, your circumcision becomes uncircumcision" (Rom. 2:25). "[I]f you accept circumcision, Christ will be of no advantage to you. I testify again to every man who accepts circumcision that he is obligated to keep the whole law" (Gal. 5:2-3). If circumcision was a sign and seal of the Covenant of Grace, then the Lord Jesus and the Apostle Paul misspoke when they equated circumcision with the Mosaic Law.

Fifth, in Romans 3, Paul teaches that the physical seed of Abraham were privileged to have the gospel (Rom. 3:1-2), but ontologically and soteriologically they were no better off than the Gentiles who were condemned by the law (Rom. 3:9-18).

Therefore, the physical seed of Abraham could not have been born into the Covenant of Grace, as some suppose, since Paul clearly states that the physical seed of Abraham were under the curse of the Covenant of Works (Rom. 3:19-20).

Again, if the blessings were unconditional for the physical seed in the Abrahamic Covenant, then it would have been unjust for God to make those same blessings conditional in the Mosaic Covenant. However, if the Abrahamic Covenant had already placed the physical children of Abraham under the obligation to obey the law of God, then the Mosaic Covenant did no injustice to the Israelites. The Mosaic Covenant simply added clarity to what was already demanded of them in the Abrahamic Covenant.

Conclusion

In seeking to comprehend the relationship between the Old and New Covenants, it is vital that we understand that the Abrahamic Covenant, although promising the Covenant of Grace, was a conditional covenant that was established with the physical seed of Abraham. The condition of the Abrahamic Covenant was clarified and codified in the Mosaic Covenant, and the gospel that was promised in the Abrahamic Covenant was contingent upon the fulfillment of the law of the Mosaic Covenant.

We have seen that there are two seeds of Abraham: one was physical and under the obligation of the Covenant of Works; the other is spiritual and have inherited the promises of the gospel. In the next chapter, we will discover more about how the physical seed of Abraham inherited the Mosaic Covenant of Works and that the Mosaic Covenant reiterated requirements already placed on Abraham's physical seed.

4

Abraham's Physical Seed

The physical seed of Abraham, independent of faith, were always under the covenantal obligation to keep the law. The blessings of the Abrahamic Covenant were dependent upon the establishment of perfect righteousness. The Mosaic Covenant did not change this requirement. The Mosaic Covenant, due to its condition, breakability, and curses was clearly a Covenant of Works. The condition is seen in the phase "do and live," the breakability is evident in Israel's unrighteousness, and the curses are manifested in the house of Israel being abandoned ("cut off") by God (1 Kings 9:6-9; Matt. 23:38).

Therefore, the promises of the Mosaic Covenant were the same as the promises of the Abrahamic Covenant: land, kingship, and a people for God (Deut. 17:14-20; 28:1-14). Just like the Abrahamic Covenant, the blessings of the promised kingdom were contingent upon the obedience of Abraham's physical seed.

The Mosaic Covenant Was Conditional

The wording of the Mosaic Covenant clearly reveals its conditional nature: "Now therefore, if you will indeed obey my voice and keep my covenant, you shall be my treasured possession among all peoples, for all the earth is mine; and you shall be to me a kingdom of priests and a holy nation" (Ex. 19:5-6a). "You shall follow my rules and keep my statutes and walk in them. I am the LORD your God. You shall therefore keep my statutes and my rules; if a person does them, he shall live by them" (Lev. 18:4-5a). "But this command I gave them: 'Obey my voice, and I will be your God, and you shall be my people. And walk in all the way that I command you, that it may be well with you'" (Jer. 7:23).

Not only did the wording of the covenant itself reveal its conditional nature, but Christ Jesus also confirmed that the Mosaic Covenant was a Covenant of Works. When a lawyer—an expert in the Mosaic Law—approached the Lord to ask what he must do to inherit eternal life, rather than giving him a direct answer, the Lord responded by asking a question in return: "What is written in the Law? How do you read it?" (Lk. 10:26). Christ was asking, in other words, how does a person inherit eternal life according to the Law of Moses?

The lawyer answered, "You shall love the Lord your God with all your heart and with all your soul and with all your strength and with all your mind, and your neighbor as yourself" (Lk. 10:27). Rather than disagreeing with this interpretation of the Mosaic law, Christ agreed with him and said, "You have answered correctly; do this, and you will live" (Lk. 10:28).

Thus, according to the terms of the Mosaic Covenant, eternal life was dependent upon the establishment of perfect righteousness.[1] "And it will be righteousness for us, if we are

---

[1] Although chapter one speaks of the Mosaic Covenant as a merely temporal and typological covenant, we shall see in chapter five that this is not because it did not promise spiritual and eternal realities (eternal life), but because it was ineffectual in establishing these spiritual and eternal realities.

careful to do all this commandment before the LORD our God, as he has commanded us" (Deut. 6:25). The covenant promised life for those who obeyed (Lev. 18:4-5) but a curse to those who disobeyed (Deut. 27:26).[2] For this reason, after reviewing the terms of the covenant, Meredith Kline rightly stated that the Mosaic Covenant "made inheritance to be by law, not by promise—not by faith, but by works."[3]

The Mosaic Covenant Contained Curses

Moreover, not only did the Mosaic Covenant contain blessings based on obedience, it also contained curses based on disobedience. "Cursed be anyone who does not confirm the words of this law by doing them" (Deut. 27:26a). The New Testament echoes this point: "Cursed be everyone who does not abide by all things written in the Book of the Law, and do them" (Gal. 3:10b).

---

[2] Greg Nichols (*Covenant Theology*, Birmingham, AL: Solid Ground Christian Books, 2011) argues that the Mosaic Covenant was a covenant of grace due to the gospel being present in the writings of Moses. He chiefly appeals to Deut. 30:9-10 in which Moses provides hope for a circumcised heart for those who repent. Nichols also refers to Rom. 3:21-22 as additional proof, but this passage is contrasting the Law of Moses and the gospel of Christ (see my explanation of this passage on pages 112-114). Nevertheless, Nichols admits that the Mosaic Covenant was not: "'if you repent and believe, then you will be my special people,' but, 'if you keep my law, then you will be my special people'" (233). By this reasoning, to say the Old Covenant is a covenant of grace because the gospel is revealed in the Old Covenant is the same as saying the New Covenant is a Covenant of Works because the condemnation of the law is revealed in the New Testament. Furthermore, Nichols contradicts himself. He attempts to justify his position by claiming the legal conditions of the Mosaic Law were necessary for sanctification (234), but he had previously claimed the New Covenant is superior to the Old Covenant because the former does not have the legal conditions of the latter (230). However, if the conditions of the Old Covenant pertained merely to sanctification, then there would be no point in dropping them from the New Covenant.

[3] Meredith Kline, *By Oath Consigned* (Grand Rapids: Eerdmans, 1968), 23.

After explaining the conditions of the covenant, Moses warned Israel of the awful consequences of disobeying the law:

> See, I am setting before you today a blessing and a curse: the blessing, if you obey the commandments of the LORD your God, which I command you today, and the curse, if you do not obey the commandments of the LORD your God, but turn aside from the way that I am commanding you today (Deut. 11:26-28a).

Being a prophet, Moses reinforced his warnings by stressing the certainty of these curses:

> The whole commandment that I command you today you shall be careful to do, that you may live and multiply, and go in and possess the land that the LORD swore to give to your fathers... Take care lest you forget the LORD your God by not keeping his commandments and his rules and his statutes, which I command you today... And if you forget the LORD your God and go after other gods and serve them and worship them, I solemnly warn you today that you shall surely perish. Like the nations that the LORD makes to perish before you, so shall you perish, because you would not obey the voice of the LORD your God (Deut. 8:1, 11, 19-20).

Jeremiah reaffirmed the conditional nature of the Mosaic Covenant and its dreadful curses:

> Hear the words of this covenant, and speak to the men of Judah and the inhabitants of Jerusalem. You shall say to them, Thus says the LORD, the God of Israel: Cursed be the man who does not hear the words of this covenant that I commanded your fathers when I brought them out of the land of Egypt, from the iron furnace, saying, Listen to my voice, and do all that I command you. So shall you be my people, and I will be your God (Jer. 11:2-4).

We find an inventory of all these dreadful curses in Deuteronomy 28. Halfway through this lengthy list, Moses warned Israel, "All these curses shall come upon you and pursue you and overtake you till you are destroyed, because you did not obey the voice of the LORD your God, to keep his commandments and his statutes that he commanded you" (Deut. 28:45). After Moses uttered all the curses, Scripture concludes, "These are the words of the covenant that the LORD commanded Moses to make with the people of Israel" (Deut. 29:1a).

The Mosaic Covenant Promised Life and Death

Calvin was correct when he wrote, "It is quite certain that the primary promises, which contained that covenant ratified with the Israelites by God under the Old Testament, were spiritual and referred to eternal life."[4] This is due to the fact that the curses of the Old Covenant not only threatened Israel with expulsion from the land of Canaan, but ultimately it also threatened the physical seed of Abraham with being "cut off" from God. For it is written, "the curses written in this book will settle upon him, and the LORD will blot out his name from under heaven" (Deut. 29:20b).[5] The Land of Promise was to be more than a geographic plot of land for the children of Israel to inhabit; more importantly, it was to be the place where God's presence would dwell with man. Therefore, to be cut

---

[4] John Calvin, *Institutes of the Christian Religion.* Edited by John T. McNeill. Translated by Ford Lewis Battles. The Library of Christian Classics (Philadelphia: Westminster Press, 1977), 4.16.11.

[5] This is not to say that the Mosaic Covenant did not also bring natural restraints and physical, temporal blessings upon Israel. Yet, this principle is applicable to any nation (or person) that upholds and enforces a standard of morality: "Righteousness exalts a nation, but sin is a reproach to any people" (Pr. 14:34).

off and exiled from the land implied the far more serious spiritual reality of being cut off and exiled from God Himself.

According to Moses, the reward for obedience was not merely a prosperous temporal life but eternal life: "You shall therefore keep my statutes and my rules; if a person does them, he shall live by them..." (Lev. 18:5a). The apostle Paul understood Moses to be speaking of eternal life when he compared and contrasted the Mosaic Covenant with the New Covenant:

> For Moses writes about the righteousness that is based on the law, that the person who does the commandments shall live by them. But the righteousness based on faith says... For with the heart one believes and is justified, and with the mouth one confesses and is saved (Rom. 10:5, 10).

In other words, Paul is not making a distinction between the "life" that was promised in the Mosaic Covenant and the "life" that is promised in the New Covenant; rather, he is contrasting how "life" was to be obtained in the Mosaic Covenant from how "life" is obtained in the New Covenant, which is a distinction between works of the law and faith in Christ Jesus. As Paul says elsewhere, "But the law is not of faith, rather 'The one who does them shall live by them'" (Gal. 3:12).

Moreover, when a certain person came up to Christ asking, "Teacher, what good deed must I do to have *eternal life*?" The Lord responded by saying, "If you would *enter life*, keep the commandments" (Matt. 19:16-17).[6] Even the Lord Jesus affirmed that it was not merely a long physical life, but eternal life, that the law of Moses promised to those who loved God with all their hearts and loved their neighbor as themselves (Lk. 10:25-28). This conversely affirms that eternal death

---

[6] Emphasis mine.

awaits the one who fails in the slightest to love God with all his heart, soul, strength, and mind.

Thus, Samuel Petto (1624-1711) concluded:

> Now the Sinai covenant is a platform of the legal righteousness which was indispensably necessary unto life; there it is deciphered, delineated, and described, more clearly than in any other federal expressure. The Sinai covenant excels all other, in discovering what that righteousness is, upon which we enjoy *eternal life*.[7]

Because the Mosaic Covenant was a republication or re-proclamation of the moral law of God, it, by necessity, promised eternal life for all who perfectly obeyed Him. Unless the Law of Moses was something less than the perfect moral law of God, it held out eternal life for those who kept it and eternal death for those who did not. As Nehemiah Coxe stated,

> This must also not be forgotten: that as Moses' law in some way included the covenant of creation and served for a memorial of it (on which account all mankind was involved in its curse), it had not only the sanction of a curse awfully denounced against the disobedient, but also a promise of the reward of life to the obedient. Now as the law of Moses was the same in moral precept with the law of creation, so the reward in this respect proposed was not a new reward, but the same that by compact had been due to Adam, in the case of his perfect obedience.[8]

According to Coxe, the promise of the Mosaic Covenant was eternal life. "Yes, such is his infinite bounty that he has proposed no lower end to his covenant transactions with men

---

[7] Samuel Petto, *The Great Mystery of the Covenant of Grace* (Stoke-on-Trent, UK: Tentmaker Publishers), 129. Emphasis is mine.
[8] Petto, *The Great Mystery of the Covenant of Grace*, 129.

than to bring them into a blessed state in the eternal enjoyment of himself."[9] Likewise, John Owen claimed: "The Old Covenant, in the preceptive part of it, renewed the commands of the Covenant of Works, and that on their original terms. Sin it forbade, that is, all and every sin, in matter and manner, on the pain of death; and gave the promise of life to perfect, sinless obedience only."[10]

If the Covenant of Works, which was given to Adam and all those in Adam, is still active with its demands and threats, and it is not unjust for God to remind a select group of Adam's fallen descendants (i.e., the children of Israel) that they are still bound by the law. Though it is impossible to obey, it is not unjust for God to remind Israel that there is no (eternal) life without the fulfillment of the law.

Just because it was impossible for the physical seed of Abraham to fulfill such a strict and demanding covenant did

---

[9] Coxe continues, "And therefore, when one covenant (through the weakness of man in his lapsed state) has been found weak and unprofitable as to this great end of a covenant because insufficient to accomplish it, God finds fault, abolishes it, and introduces another in which full provision is made for the perfect salvation of those that have interest in it (Hebrews 8:7, 8)" (*Covenant Theology*, 37).

[10] *Covenant Theology*, 202. Because the Old Covenant included a revival of the original Covenant of Works, I also agree with John Owen that it "did never save nor condemn any man eternally. All that lived under the administration of it did attain eternal life, or perished for ever, but not by virtue of this covenant as formally such. It did, indeed, revive the commanding power and sanction of the first Covenant of Works; and in that respect, as the apostle speaks, was 'the ministry of condemnation,' 2 Cor. 3:9; for 'by the deeds of the law can no flesh be justified.' And on the other hand, it directed also to the promise, which was the instrument of life and salvation to all that did believe. But as to what it had of its own, it was confined to things temporal. Believers were saved under it, but not by virtue of it. Sinners perished eternally under it, but by the curse of the original law of works" (*Covenant Theology*, 197-198). Since all were already condemned in Adam, none could be justified or condemned by the Mosaic Covenant in and of itself. Therefore, for sinners, the Mosaic Covenant was restricted to merely temporal and typological blessings. (For further explanation, see pages 99-105).

not mean its promises and curses were nullified.[11] The Israelites' responsibility to obey was not contingent upon their ability to obey. This may seem unfair, but the moral law, by its very nature, cannot be anything but fair. Because of their inability to keep the demands of the Mosaic Covenant, the Mosaic Covenant is said to be an administration unto death rather than unto life, for "by works of the law no one will be justified" (Gal. 2:16; cf. Rom. 3:20). "For although in itself," John Owen remarked, "it requires a perfect righteousness, and gives a promise of life for that reason, ('He that does these things, he will live in them,') yet it could give neither righteousness nor life to any in the state of sin."[12]

Though it was impossible for sinners to obey the Mosaic Covenant, its blessings and curses were not merely hypothetical. The Covenant of Works condemns all those who are not found righteous in the sight of God. Hell is proof that the terms of the Covenant of Works are unchangeable. The death of Christ on the cross is proof that the requirements of the covenant were not hypothetical.

For the blessings of the law to be established, the physical seed of Abraham (i.e., Christ) had to fulfill the demands and the curses of the law. This is the only way in which God could be both just and merciful. Thus, for sinners, the Mosaic Law was given to awaken them to their own sinfulness and administer death, but for the righteous (i.e., Christ) it was given to reveal and establish life.

---

[11] According to Edward Fisher, the inability to obey the Mosaic Covenant did not make the covenant unjust: "[F]or the Lord may justly require perfect obedience at all men's hands, by virtue of that covenant which was made with them in Adam; and if any man could yield perfect obedience to the law, both in doing and suffering, he should have eternal life; for we may not deny (says Calvin) but that the reward of eternal salvation belongeth to the upright obedience of the law" (*The Marrow of Modern Divinity*, 85).

[12] Coxe and Owen, *Covenant Theology*, 193.

The Failure of Abraham's Physical Seed

Life and death were at stake in the Mosaic Covenant. After hearing the terms of the covenant, the nation of Israel agreed to keep the condition, "All that the LORD has spoken we will do" (Ex. 19:8; Ex. 24:3). It is important to note that Israel still would have still been under the law even if they had disagreed with the terms of the covenant, for they were already guilty in Adam. Nevertheless, their quick response revealed a blindness to their own inward depravity.

Although they agreed to the terms, the actual history of Israel demonstrates their complete and utter failure to obey God. This failure, from the very beginning, was signified when Moses broke the two tablets of stone bearing the law. Israel broke the covenant as soon as they agreed to keep the covenant, as it is written: "They have turned aside quickly out of the way that I commanded them" (Ex. 32:8).

From the beginning, Israel broke God's law. From the beginning, God blinded them and gave them over to a heart of unbelief so that, when Moses came down from the mountain, he was forced to veil himself because, as Paul declared, "their minds were hardened." Moses realized this, for he tells them, "But to this day the LORD has not given you a heart to understand or eyes to see or ears to hear" (Deut. 29:4). Earlier, Moses stated, "Furthermore, the LORD said to me, 'I have seen this people, and behold, it is a stubborn people. Let me alone, that I may destroy them and blot out their name from under heaven'" (Deut. 9:13-14a). "And he said, 'I will hide my face from them; I will see what their end will be, for they are a perverse generation, children in whom is no faithfulness'" (Deut. 32:20).

The author of Hebrews confirms this truth:

I was provoked with that generation, and said, 'They always go astray in their heart; they have not known my ways.' As I swore in my wrath, 'They shall not enter my rest.'" [...] And to whom did he swear that they would not enter his rest, but to those who were disobedient? So we see that they were unable to enter because of unbelief (Heb. 3:10-11, 18-19).

Not only did the charter members of the Mosaic Covenant walk the paths of ungodliness, but Israel's succeeding generations continued to also march down the same idolatrous road of unbelief and disobedience. From Moses to Samuel, Israel remained disobedient to their covenantal commitment. For instance, after Israel demanded a king, the Lord brought forth this indictment against them:

And the LORD said to Samuel, "Obey the voice of the people in all that they say to you, for they have not rejected you, but they have rejected me from being king over them. According to all the deeds that they have done, from the day I brought them up out of Egypt even to this day, forsaking me and serving other gods, so they are also doing to you (1 Sam. 8:7-8).

Throughout their history, the children of Israel never improved. Therefore, God commissioned Isaiah, "Make the heart of this people dull, and their ears heavy, and blind their eyes; lest they see with their eyes, and hear with their ears, and understand with their hearts, and turn and be healed" (Isa. 6:10). "But my people did not listen to my voice; Israel would not submit to me. So I gave them over to their stubborn hearts, to follow their own counsels" (Ps. 81:11-12).

Amos, a contemporary of Isaiah, cried out against Judah as well:

Thus says the LORD: "For three transgressions of Judah, and for four, I will not revoke the punishment, because they have rejected the law of the LORD, and have not kept his statutes, but their lies have led them astray, those after which their fathers walked" (Amos 2:4).

The Lord, speaking through the prophet Isaiah, again characterized Israel as a wicked and ungodly nation:

> Hear, O heavens, and give ear, O earth; for the LORD has spoken: "Children have I reared and brought up, but they have rebelled against me." [...] Ah, sinful nation, a people laden with iniquity, offspring of evildoers, children who deal corruptly! They have forsaken the LORD, they have despised the Holy One of Israel, they are utterly estranged (Isa. 1:2, 4).

There was not a single command that Israel did not break. Prior to the Assyrian exile, God placed this indictment upon the children of Abraham:

> And this occurred because the people of Israel had sinned against the LORD their God, who had brought them up out of the land of Egypt from under the hand of Pharaoh king of Egypt, and had feared other gods and walked in the customs of the nations whom the LORD drove out before the people of Israel, and in the customs that the kings of Israel had practiced. And the people of Israel did secretly against the LORD their God things that were not right. They built for themselves high places in all their towns, from watchtower to fortified city. They set up for themselves pillars and Asherim on every high hill and under every green tree, and there they made offerings on all the high places, as the nations did whom the LORD carried away before them. And they did wicked things, provoking the LORD to anger, and they served idols, of which the LORD had said to them, "You shall not do this." Yet the LORD warned Israel and Judah by every prophet and every seer, saying, "Turn from your evil ways and keep my commandments and my

statutes, in accordance with all the Law that I commanded your fathers, and that I sent to you by my servants the prophets."

But they would not listen, but were stubborn, as their fathers had been, who did not believe in the LORD their God. They despised his statutes and his covenant that he made with their fathers and the warnings that he gave them. They went after false idols and became false, and they followed the nations that were around them, concerning whom the LORD had commanded them that they should not do like them. And they abandoned all the commandments of the LORD their God, and made for themselves metal images of two calves; and they made an Asherah and worshiped all the host of heaven and served Baal. And they burned their sons and their daughters as offerings and used divination and omens and sold themselves to do evil in the sight of the LORD, provoking him to anger (2 Kings 17:7-17).

A few years afterwards, Jeremiah repeated this charge against Israel:

For I solemnly warned your fathers when I brought them up out of the land of Egypt, warning them persistently, even to this day, saying, Obey my voice. Yet they did not obey or incline their ear, but everyone walked in the stubbornness of his evil heart. Therefore I brought upon them all the words of this covenant, which I commanded them to do, but they did not" (Jer. 11:7-8).

Looking back upon the fathers of the Old Covenant, Jeremiah referred to them as disobedient covenant breakers.

Again the LORD said to me, "A conspiracy exists among the men of Judah and the inhabitants of Jerusalem. They have turned back to the iniquities of their forefathers, who refused to hear my words. They have gone after other gods to serve them. The house of Israel and the house of Judah have broken my covenant that I made with their fathers. Therefore, thus says the LORD, Behold, I am bringing disaster upon them that they cannot escape. Though they cry to me, I will not listen to them" (Jer. 11:9-11).

Daniel, seventy years later, confirmed this accusation against the physical seed of Abraham (Dan. 9:11). Even after returning from exile, Israel did not improve. After learning that Israelites had not kept themselves pure, but rather had married into the pagan nations, Ezra made this confession before God:

> O my God, I am ashamed and blush to lift my face to you, my God, for our iniquities have risen higher than our heads, and our guilt has mounted up to the heavens. From the days of our fathers to this day we have been in great guilt. And for our iniquities we, our kings, and our priests have been given into the hand of the kings of the lands, to the sword, to captivity, to plundering, and to utter shame, as it is today. [...] And now, O our God, what shall we say after this? For we have forsaken your commandments (Ezra 9:6-7, 10).

From Ezra to the close of the Old Testament canon, this ungodly people continued to ignore their covenantal commitment. One of the last things God said to the Jews, preceding the 400 years of silence, was that they had been and remained a disobedient people: "From the days of your fathers you have turned aside from my statutes and have not kept them" (Mal. 3:7a).

John Owen vividly summarized the idolatry of Old Testament Israel in this way:

> In a word, there was nothing so vile or so wicked, nothing so obscene or so filthy ever devised by the most accursed and mindless of idolaters (or suggested to them by the prince of darkness) which they did not, at length, choose in

place of the most chaste and holy worship of the one living God.[13]

In Acts 7, Stephen preached a sermon in which he affirmed the testimony of Moses, Samuel, Amos, Isaiah, Malachi, and the rest of the prophets. Preaching to the leaders of Israel, Stephen gives an overall synopsis of the history of the Jewish people from Abraham onward, summarizing many key events. In all of this, his focus was on Israel's continuous and current rebellion. The climax of his message came when he charged the current leaders of Israel with the same disobedience that characterized their fathers:

> You stiff-necked people, uncircumcised in heart and ears, you always resist the Holy Spirit. As your fathers did, so do you. Which of the prophets did not your fathers persecute? And they killed those who announced beforehand the coming of the Righteous One, whom you have now betrayed and murdered, you who received the law as delivered by angels and did not keep it (Acts 7:51-53).

Not only was this Stephen's understanding, but it was also that of the apostle Paul. In his letter to the Romans, Paul claimed that Israel had always been and remained "a disobedient and contrary people" (Rom. 10:21). Therefore, Paul claimed: "God gave them a spirit of stupor, eyes that would not see and ears that would not hear, down to this very day. ...let their eyes be darkened so that they cannot see, and bend their backs forever" (Rom. 11:8, 10). This was the reason Paul would turn his missionary efforts to the Gentiles:

> The Holy Spirit was right in saying to your fathers through Isaiah the prophet: "'Go to this people, and say, 'You will indeed hear but never understand, and you will indeed see

---

[13] John Owen, *Biblical Theology* (Morgan, PA: Soli Deo Gloria, 2002), 445.

but never perceive.' For this people's heart has grown dull, and with their ears they can barely hear, and their eyes they have closed; lest they should see with their eyes and hear with their ears and understand with their heart and turn, and I would heal them." Therefore let it be known to you that this salvation of God has been sent to the Gentiles; they will listen' (Acts 28:25-28).

The Mosaic Covenant Was Broken

The physical seed of Abraham were obligated to obey God. Yet as we have seen, they were unable to keep their commitment to the covenant: "They did not keep God's covenant, but refused to walk according to his law" (Ps. 78:10). As the prophet Hosea recorded, "But like Adam they transgressed the covenant" (Hos. 6:7). Jeremiah acknowledged this as well: "The house of Israel and the house of Judah have broken my covenant that I made with their fathers. Therefore, thus says the LORD, Behold, I am bringing disaster upon them that they cannot escape" (Jer. 11:10-11). The physical seed of Abraham were unable to keep the law (Rom. 3:9-18). As Peter concluded, the yoke of the law was too heavy for them to bear (Acts 15:10).

The Preservation of Abraham's Physical Seed

The question remains, if the physical seed of Abraham were marked by continual disobedience, why did God continue to bestow mercy and longsuffering upon them? How could the physical seed of Abraham have been under the Covenant of Works and yet continue to receive mercy from the hands of a just God? The answer is not that they were the physical offspring of Abraham, for their ethnicity did not impress God (Matt. 3:9).

Rather, the only thing that saved the children of Israel from being destroyed in the wilderness—or throughout the entire history of the Old Testament—was the unconditional promise God had made to Abraham. God's faithfulness was what preserved the Jews. God promised the Messiah would be the physical child of Abraham. In spite of Israel's disobedience and unfaithfulness, God was committed to keeping the genealogical line of Abraham alive, at least until the promised seed was born. "And as Isaiah said before: 'Unless the LORD of Sabaoth had left us a seed, We would have become like Sodom, And we would have been made like Gomorrah" (Rom. 9:29 NKJV).

The preservation of Israel was vital to keep the genealogical line of Christ alive. In other words, it was the promise of the Abrahamic Covenant (*in your seed all the nations of the earth will be blessed*) that preserved the physical seed of Abraham. As Michael Horton explained, "[W]henever God shows leniency by not executing the curses of the covenant upon Israel's transgression, the basis of such leniency is never the Sinaitic covenant itself, but the Abrahamic (or Davidic (cf. 2 Kings 13:23). There is no mercy in the Sinaitic covenant itself."[14] This is in agreement with the Scriptures: "But the LORD was gracious to them and had compassion on them, and he turned toward them, because of his covenant with Abraham, Isaac, and Jacob, and would not destroy them, nor has he cast them from his presence until now" (2 Kings 13:23). Because Judah was the progenitor of the Messiah, the Jews were saved from being completely "cut off" by the Covenant of Works.

For clarity's sake, it was not the condition but the promise of the Abrahamic Covenant that preserved Israel. Even prior

---

[14] Horton, *God of Promise*, 50.

to the establishment of the Mosaic Covenant, the preservation of the physical children of Abraham was tied to the promise.[15]

Nevertheless, the problem with the physical seed of Abraham was not that they were unable to keep the Covenant of Works. Instead, their failure was that they did not trust in the promise that God gave them. They should have known it was impossible to fulfill the law. The law was given to show them their sins. Because of their sins, they should have trusted all the more in the Abrahamic promise. They should have been looking for the promised seed (i.e., Christ) rather than thinking they could keep the law.

The Unbelief of Abraham's Physical Seed

Thus, their problem was not a lack of obedience but a lack of faith. They failed to believe because they took pride in the fact that they were the circumcised children of Abraham (Matt. 3:9). They placed too much confidence in their moral ability.

It seems many Jews of Jesus' day viewed the law as only commanding external conformity rather than demanding purity of the heart. Therefore, with a high view of them- selves and a low view of the law, they sought to establish their own righteousness by works rather than by submitting to the righteousness of Christ by faith (Rom. 10:3-4).

They were given the law to lead them to repentance and faith in Christ, but they skipped over the unconditional promise (i.e., Christ) by trying to fulfill the conditional requirement of the covenant themselves. They tried to live by the law that can only bring death to sinners (Rom. 7:10). Rather than looking at their sacrificial system and concluding

---

[15] The failure to comprehend the dichotomous nature of the Abrahamic Covenant is where New Perspective on Paul begins to go astray. See Appendix.

that they needed a substitute, they trusted in themselves. Rather than submitting to the righteousness of Christ by faith, a righteousness that fulfills the Covenant of Works, they tried to fulfill the Covenant of Works for themselves by trusting in their ethnicity and their moral ability to fulfill the works of the law.

What Christ was called to do as the seed of Abraham, the Jews thought they could do as the seed of Abraham. Consequently, their unbelief was the leading cause of their demise. In short, they should have trusted in the Messiah who would fulfill Abrahamic promise rather than thinking that they themselves were its fulfillment.

The "Cutting Off" of Abraham's Physical Seed

The coming of the Messiah, the promised seed of Abraham, should have been a joyous event, but the Jews were too prideful to have their promised King rule over them. Though the kingdom was at hand, the physical seed of Abraham remained blinded in unbelief—even in the face of this overwhelmingly good news. They were too prideful to submit to an alien righteousness. They rejected the very cornerstone they should have built their life upon. They turned against their promised King, their own Messiah, and had Him crucified.

As a result, all that remained for those who rejected Christ was to be rejected and "cut off" from God and His people (Matt. 23:38; Gal. 4:30). Moses predicted Israel's demise from the beginning: "The LORD will send on you curses...until you are destroyed..." (Deut. 28:20). Jeremiah reaffirmed the certainty of the execution of the curses of the law upon Israel:

> I will make you a horror to all the kingdoms of the earth.
> And the men who transgressed my covenant and did not

keep the terms of the covenant that they made before me, I will make them like the calf that they cut in two and passed between its parts – the officials of Judah, the officials of Jerusalem, the eunuchs, the priests, and all the people of the land who passed between the parts of the calf. And I will give them into the hand of their enemies and into the hand of those who seek their lives. Their dead bodies shall be food for the birds of the air and the beasts of the earth (Jer. 34:17-20).

This caused Isaiah to lament Israel's failure:

Oh that you had paid attention to my commandments! Then your peace would have been like a river, and your righteousness like the waves of the sea; your offspring would have been like the sand, and your descendants like its grains; their names would never be cut off or destroyed from before me (Isa. 48:18-19).

Yet, once the promised seed of Abraham arrived with the birth of Jesus, it was no longer necessary to keep the genealogical line of Abraham alive. Therefore, the dreadful curses of the Abrahamic and Mosaic Covenants would be unleashed upon Israel in full. The kingdom that was promised to them would be given to the Gentiles (Matt. 8:11-12; 21:43) and the curses of the covenant would be executed upon Israel. As Christ boldly pronounced: "See, your house [racial lineage] is left to you desolate" (Matt. 23:38).

As the author of Hebrews claimed: "For they did not continue in my covenant, and so I showed no concern for them, declares the Lord" (Heb. 8:9). Therefore, Paul stated that the "wrath [of God] has come upon them [the Jews] at last!" (1 Thess. 2:16).

Conclusion

Although there was a small remnant of the physical seed of Abraham that were saved by grace through faith in the promise of the Abrahamic Covenant, the bulk of Abraham's physical children would die in their sin and unbelief. A select few were brought into the Covenant of Grace by becoming Abraham's spiritual seed by faith, but most of the physical children of Israel proved themselves not to be among the true Israel of God (Rom. 9:6). In short, the physical children of Abraham were placed under a condition which they were unable to fulfill, and their history is marked by disobedience, unbelief, and idolatry.

5

Abraham's Spiritual Seed

"The kingdom of God is at hand," is the message that opens the New Testament. The long-awaited fulfillment of the Abrahamic Covenant was drawing nigh, according to John the Baptist. Long ago, the Abrahamic Covenant had promised the establishment of the kingdom of God, and 400 years later, the Mosaic Covenant, with greater clarity, explained the high cost of the kingdom. Yet, thousands of years would pass without any fulfillment of the promise because none of Abraham's children were able to fulfill the condition of the kingdom. That is, none until the birth of the promised seed of Abraham—Jesus Christ.

According to the Mosaic Covenant, the kingdom was predicated upon the establishment of perfect righteousness (Ex. 19:3-6). It was for this reason that Jesus Christ preached the gospel of the kingdom; a gospel that would redeem God's people from their sins and establish the righteousness needed for the promised seed (Christ Himself) to take dominion over the true people of God.

The Purpose of the Law

It becomes evident that the Mosaic Covenant was not parenthetically inserted into the history of redemption. Nor was it merely typological in nature. Rather, the Law of Moses was a crucial and necessary part of the story of redemption. For without the satisfaction of the law, there would be no salvation.

The law was given to Israel for various reasons. As is already mentioned, the law fully explained what circumcision implied. In addition, the law was a natural means of safeguarding the physical seed of Abraham. Sin causes any people group or nation to self-destruct. The Mosaic Covenant not only organized Abraham's physical children into a nation but also brought natural restraints. For instance, many of the ceremonial laws were designed to place a fence around Israel. These laws (e.g., dietary laws) separated the Jews from the Gentiles. Moreover, the law was given to prevent Israel from intermarrying and thus being absorbed into other nations which would have diluted the genealogical line of Christ.

One of the more important purposes of the law, according to Paul, was to expose sin in the sinner. The law was designed to show the physical seed of Abraham that they were already covenant breakers and under the wrath of God. The law was to point the Israelites away from themselves and to faith in the coming Messiah. For these reasons, the law was an important precursor to the gospel.

Of all these purposes, the most important purpose of the law was to bring about the legal righteousness that was needed for the seed of Abraham to establish the promised kingdom of God (Ex. 19:3-6; Deut. 6:25). Since Adam had broken the Covenant of Works, the only hope was for the seed of the woman to fulfill it instead. Therefore, Christ, the seed of the woman and of Abraham, was born under the law so He could accomplish what Adam failed to achieve. Samuel Petto realized this when he stated:

> The Covenant of Works being broken by us in the first Adam, it was of great concernment to us that satisfaction should be given to it, for unless its righteousness were performed for us, the promised life was unattainable; and unless its penalty were undergone for us, the threatened death (Gen. ii.17.) was unavoidable.[1]

It is important to note that the moral requirements that God established with Abraham and Moses are the same as the requirements that God established with Adam, for it consisted of the same moral law, accompanied by the same blessings and curses. Eschatological life and death were at the heart of both. In this regards, the Mosaic Covenant was not a New Covenant of Works, but a re-proclamation of the Covenant of Works that was previously established with Adam. As Edward Fisher writes, "the law delivered on Mount Sinai, and formerly engraven on man's heart, was one and the same; so that at Mount Sinai the Lord delivered no new thing."[2]

In addition, John Owen stated,

> [The Mosaic Covenant] revived the sanction of the first covenant, in the curse or sentence of death which is denounced against all transgression. Death was the penalty of the transgression of the first covenant: "In the day that you eat of it, you will die the death." And this sentence was revived and represented anew in the curse by which this

---

[1] Petto, *The Great Mystery of the Covenant of Grace*, 126.
[2] Edward Fisher, *The Marrow of Modern Divinity* (Ross-shire, UK: Christian Focus, 2009), 80.

covenant was ratified, "Cursed be he that confirms not all the words of this law to do them."[3]

Therefore, these two covenants are one in principle. Since Christ was born of the Virgin Mary, He did not inherit the twofold curse (guilt and depravity) of the broken covenant of creation. However, He was still born under the law that had been republished in both the Abrahamic and Mosaic Covenants. The moral law broken by the first Adam was the same moral law which was satisfied by the second Adam (Rom. 5:12-21).

Adam, acting as federal head of the human race, broke the Covenant of Works, thereby brining death to all his descendants. Christ, acting as federal head of the elect, fulfilled the law, thereby bringing life to all who are united to Him by faith. Thus, one either stands condemned in Adam, who broke the Covenant of Works, or justified in Christ, Who fulfilled the Covenant of Works. One is either united with the first Adam, and thus under law, or united with the second Adam, and thus under grace.

This means that the Adamic Covenant, broken by Adam, is still holding Adam's natural seed captive to the curse of the law (i.e., death). With this in view, Paul explained that both Jews and Gentiles are born under the Covenant of Works (Rom. 2:12-15) and are equally condemned by it (Rom. 3:9-10).

The difference between the Jews and Gentiles, however, was that God republished the Covenant of Works with the seed of Abraham by adding additional positive laws for them to obey (Eph. 2:11-12). The purpose was not so the depraved children of Abraham could foolishly attempt to work their way

---

[3] Coxe and Owen, *Covenant Theology*, 189.

to God, but so the promised seed of Abraham (i.e., Jesus Christ) could fulfill the law and bring salvation to the nations. This is why the Lord Jesus said salvation was of the Jews and not of the Gentiles (Jn. 4:22).

It is crucial to note that if the physical seed of Abraham had been automatically born into the Covenant of Grace, as some suppose, then there would never have been any hope for fallen sinners. Why? Because by necessity this would mean that Christ, as the physical seed of Abraham, would have also been born into the Covenant of Grace, and if this were true, then He could not have been cursed by the Covenant of Works on the cross (2 Cor. 5:21; Col. 2:13-15).

Christ Has Fulfilled the Law

Thankfully, however, Christ, as with all the physical seed of Abraham, was born into the Covenant of Works so that by His active and passive obedience He could establish the New Covenant of grace for all those who would be united to Him by faith. Thus, Christ was "born under the law, to redeem those who were under the law" (Gal. 4:4-5). "Therefore," John Owen claimed, "did he [Christ], all the days of his flesh, serve God in a Covenant of Works; and was therein accepted with him, having done nothing that should disannul the virtue of that covenant as to him."[4]

This is the heart of the gospel. Without Christ's fulfillment of the law, all the promises of Abraham would also go unfulfilled, for it was evident that none of Abraham's other children was able to obey the law. For generation after generation, the children of Israel failed in the keeping of their

---

[4] John Owen, "Of Communion with God the Father, Son, and Holy Ghost," in *The Works of John Owen*. 16 vols. Edited by William H. Goold. (1965-1968. Reprint, Edinburgh, UK: Banner of Truth Trust, 2000), 2:65.

covenant obligations—until the birth of Christ. This is why Paul said that Christ endured the curse of the Mosaic Covenant in order to bring about the promise of the Abrahamic Covenant:

> For all who rely on works of the law [the Mosaic Covenant] are under a curse; for it is written, "Cursed be everyone who does not abide by all things written in the Book of the Law, and do them." Now it is evident that no one is justified before by the law [the Mosaic Covenant], for "The righteous shall live by faith." But the law is not of faith, rather "The one who does them shall live by them." Christ redeemed us from the curse of the law by becoming a curse for us—for it is written, "Cursed is everyone who is hanged on a tree"— so that in Christ Jesus the blessing of Abraham might come to the Gentiles, so that we might receive the promised Spirit through faith. (Gal. 3:10-14)

However, Christ was the One Whom God had in mind the whole time: "Now the promises were made to Abraham and to his offspring. It does not say, 'And to offsprings,' referring to many, but referring to one, 'And to your offspring,' who is Christ" (Gal. 3:16).

Israel's disobedience did not nullify God's faithfulness to His promises even though the conditions of the Mosaic had to be satisfied in order for the promises of the Abraham Covenant to be fulfilled. As Paul wrote, "Does their faithlessness nullify the faithfulness of God? By no means!" (Rom. 3:3-4). God kept His promise to Abraham by sending Christ Jesus. As it is written, "But when the fullness of time had come, God sent forth His Son, born of woman, born under the law, to redeem those who were under the law..." (Gal. 4:4-5). Christ did not come to do away with the law but to fulfill it (Matt. 5:17).

Christ Is the Promised Physical Seed

It is pertinent to remember the Covenant of Works is holy and eternal. Its weakness is not in the covenant itself but in its membership. Fallen man is unable to fulfill the legal and righteous demands of God's law. Yet, what fallen man cannot do, Christ was able to do.

> For God has done what the law, weakened by the flesh, could not do. By sending his own Son in the likeness of sinful flesh and for sin, he condemned sin in the flesh, in order that the righteous requirement of the law might be fulfilled in us (Rom. 8:3-4).

Jesus Christ is the ultimate fulfillment of the Abrahamic Covenant. The Lord Jesus fulfilled both the unconditional promise and the conditional requirement. Therefore, Paul made it clear that, when God made the covenant with Abraham, the promise was not referring to offsprings in the plural form, but to an offspring in the singular (Gal. 3:16). When Christ was born, the unconditional promise was fulfilled. When Christ died, the conditional requirement was fulfilled. Therefore, all of the promises reside in Christ alone.

What a wonderful plan of redemption that placed Christ, the seed of Abraham, under the law so both Jews and Gentiles can be saved in Him alone by grace alone through faith alone to the glory of God alone!

The Spiritual Seed of Abraham

This means, however, that outside of union with Christ, there is no inheritance of the blessings of the Abrahamic Covenant. Both Jews and Gentiles are born under the conditions of the Covenant of Works, and both will remain under its curses as long as they remain in unbelief, outside of union with Christ Jesus. This also means Abraham's physical children who remained outside of a saving union with Christ remained outside of the gates of the kingdom of God. In agreement with the terms of the Abrahamic Covenant, the unbelieving Jews were "cut off" from God. This is why John the Baptist warned the children of Israel not to boast in the fact that they were the children of Abraham (Matt. 3:9).

Because it was impossible for the physical children of Abraham to become the spiritual children of Abraham by the works of the law, God must have intended for there to be another way—a better way. Romans, chapter 4, explains this better way:

> Is this blessing then only for the circumcised, or also for the uncircumcised? For we say that faith was counted to Abraham as righteousness. How then was it counted to him? Was it before or after he had been circumcised? It was not after, but before he was circumcised. He received the sign of circumcision as a seal of the righteousness that he had by faith while he was still uncircumcised. The purpose was to make him the father of all who believe without being circumcised, so that righteousness would be counted to them as well, and to make him the father of the circumcised who are not merely circumcised but who also walk in the footsteps of the faith that our father Abraham had before he was circumcised. For the promise to Abraham and his offspring that he would be heir of the world did not come through the law but through the righteousness of faith (Rom. 4:9-13).

In other words, sinners are saved the same way Abraham was saved—by faith alone.

> Know then that it is those of faith who are the sons of Abraham. And the Scripture, foreseeing that God would justify the Gentiles by faith, preached the gospel beforehand to Abraham, saying, "In you shall all the nations be blessed."

So then, those who are of faith are blessed along with Abraham, the man of faith (Gal. 3:7-9).

How does faith transform physical Jews and Gentiles into the spiritual children of Abraham? As we have already seen, all the spiritual blessings of Abraham are fulfilled in Christ Jesus (Eph. 1:3). Outside of union with Christ, all physical children remain in darkness and under the curse of the Covenant of Works. Thus, faith transforms sinners into the children of Abraham by uniting them to the promised seed of Abraham—Christ Jesus. Once sinners are united to Christ by faith, they become legal heirs with Christ to all the promised blessings of Abraham:

> Christ redeemed us from the curse of the law by becoming a curse for us – for it is written, "Cursed is everyone who is hanged on a tree" – so that in Christ Jesus the blessing of Abraham might come to the Gentiles, so that we might receive the promised Spirit through faith... [I]n Christ Jesus you are all sons of God, through faith. For as many of you as were baptized into Christ have put on Christ. There is neither Jew nor Greek, there is neither slave nor free, there is no male and female, for you are all one in Christ Jesus. And if you are Christ's, then you are Abraham's offspring, heirs according to promise (Gal. 3:13-14; 26- 29).

Moreover, this was not just a New Testament phenomenon. Rather, the true children of Abraham have always consisted of those who have been born of the Spirit and inwardly circumcised in the heart. "For no one is a Jew who is merely one outwardly, nor is circumcision outward and physical. But a Jew is one inwardly, and circumcision is a matter of the heart, by the Spirit, not by the letter. His praise is not from man but from God" (Rom. 2:28-29).

Even in the Old Testament, as Paul explained, not all Israel was of spiritual Israel:

> But it is not as though the word of God has failed. For not all who are descended from Israel belong to Israel, and not all are children of Abraham because they are his offspring, but "Through Isaac shall your offspring be named." This means that it is not the children of the flesh who are the children of God, but the children of the promise are counted as offspring" (Rom. 9:6-8).

Ishmael and the rest of Abraham's children by his second wife all were the physical seed of Abraham, but they all were "cut off" from the promised inheritance. For example, Ishmael was the circumcised firstborn of Abraham, but the full inheritance went to Isaac. In the same way, Paul explained that what was true of Ishmael was equally true of all of Abraham's unbelieving physical children. Only those who are children of Abraham by faith are heirs to the promised inheritance. Like Ishmael, the rest of Abraham's unbelieving physical children have been left deserted by God (Gal. 4:28-31).

For this reason, G. H. Kersten was right when he stated that only the elect are members of the Covenant of Grace:

> [The] organic unity of the elect as the body of Christ and the spiritual offspring of Abraham, is fully revealed in the Covenant of Grace. Scripture refers to this when it speaks of the covenant established with Abraham and his seed. That was the great promise of the covenant: "I will be a God unto thee, and to thy seed after thee," not as if grace were transplanted from father to son, but rather that God would bring forth a spiritual seed out of Abraham, that is the children of promise as Isaac was...He who states that the Covenant of Grace was established with Abraham and his natural seed must include in Gen. 3:15 also the children of Keturah, indeed, all posterity of Adam and Eve in the

covenant...As this first covenant revelation did not speak of the natural seed of the woman, so this covenant does not apply to the natural seed of Abraham...The Lord established the covenant with Abraham and his spiritual seed, in other words, with the elect. They, and only they, are incorporated in the covenant.[5]

The Efficacy of the New Covenant

Therefore, the difference between the physical and spiritual seed of Abraham is that the physical seed were born into the Covenant of Works, while the spiritual seed are reborn into the Covenant of Grace.

This shows us the fundamental difference between the Old and New Covenants. Both covenants promise the same blessings and both covenants demand perfect righteousness, but only in the New Covenant of grace is the righteous requirement fulfilled in Christ. The gospel supplies what the law demands, as it is written: "Christ is the end of the law for righteousness for everyone who believes" (Rom. 10:4).

Yet the deficiency was not in the Mosaic Covenant itself, for the Old Covenant was a righteous and holy covenant. Rather, the deficiency was in the membership of the Old Covenant. The members of the Old Covenant were unable to fulfill what was demanded of them by the covenant (Rom. 8:3).

Seeing the weakness of the Old Covenant, Jeremiah predicted a New Covenant that would be able to perform within its membership what the Old Covenant could not.

> Behold, the days are coming, declares the LORD, when I will make a New Covenant with the house of Israel and the house of Judah, not like the covenant that I made with their

---

[5] G. H. Kersten, *Reformed Dogmatics*, 2 vols. (Grand Rapids: HeuleGordon, 2009), 1:247.

fathers on the day when I took them by the hand to bring them out of the land of Egypt, my covenant that they broke, though I was their husband, declares the LORD. For this is the covenant that I will make with the house of Israel after those days, declares the LORD: I will put my law within them, and I will write it on their hearts. And I will be their God, and they shall be my people. And no longer shall each one teach his neighbor and each his brother, saying, 'Know the LORD,' for they shall all know me, from the least of them to the greatest, declares the LORD. For I will forgive their iniquity, and I will remember their sin no more (Jer. 31:31-34).

Therefore, according to Jeremiah, the chief difference between the two covenants was the Old Covenant was broken while the New Covenant is unbreakable.[6] For instance, the Old Covenant featured the law written on stone, but it could not change a heart of stone. In contrast, the New Covenant writes the law upon the heart (Jer. 31:33). The Old Covenant demanded a circumcised heart, but the New Covenant supplies a circumcised heart. All unbelieving members of the Old Covenant were cut off from God, but all the members of the New Covenant are believers and are preserved in a loving, personal relationship with God (Jer. 31:34). The members of the Old Covenant were condemned by the law, but the members of the New Covenant are justified by Christ.

---

[6] Some Reformed Baptists follow the line of reasoning presented by some paedobaptists who claim the difference between the Old and New Covenants is not *qualitative* but *quantitative*. Unlike the paedobaptists, however, these Reformed Baptists stress that the quantitative difference is that "all" know the Lord in the New Covenant, as opposed to only a small remnant knowing the Lord in Old Covenant. The problem, however, is that Jeremiah is not speaking of a quantitative but a *qualitative* difference because he is contrasting the powerlessness and breakability of the Old Covenant with the unbreakable character and saving efficacy of the New Covenant. This is not merely a matter of degree, but of the essential difference between law and grace.

Those who belong to the Covenant of Works were represented by the first Adam, but those who belong to the Covenant of Grace are represented by the second Adam. In this way, the New Covenant is superior; it has a better Mediator and is based upon better promises (Heb. 8:6). Thus, Michael Horton was right when he said:

> The human race is divided no longer between Jew and Gentile, but between those who are "in Adam" (under the covenant of law) and those who are "in Christ" (in the Covenant of Grace) ... To be "in Adam" is to belong to the Covenant of Works, the transgression of which means that all those represented by Adam are under bondage to sin and death. On the other hand, to be "in Christ" is to be justified, sanctified, and glorified.[7]

It is important to note that when Scripture speaks of the Mosaic Covenant as being physical and of the New Covenant as being spiritual, this does not mean the Old Covenant was unconcerned about spiritual realities (e.g., a circumcised heart, eternal life) or that the New Covenant is unconcerned about physical realities (e.g., a new earth, a resurrected body). Rather, the difference between the Old and New Covenants is that they approach the physical and spiritual concerns of the Abrahamic Covenant from two different directions or starting points.

The Old Covenant was ineffectual because it sought to reform the inner man by external means. For instance, the Mosaic Covenant started by issuing outward circumcision, then afterwards it demanded inward circumcision. Once the Old Covenant law was etched in stone, it required inward obedience from the heart. Because the Old Covenant started

---

[7] Michael Horton, *The Christian Faith* (Grand Rapids: Zondervan, 2011), 716.

from the outside, it remained ineffectual in establishing for its unregenerate membership the spiritual promises of the Abrahamic Covenant. No matter how hard one tries, outward legislation alone (regardless of the purity of the laws) can never change sinful and depraved hearts.

On the other hand, the New Covenant is effectual in securing the physical promises of the Abrahamic Covenant because it starts, not with the physical, but with the spiritual realities. Before the saints inherit the world at the end of the age, they must receive the New Covenant blessing of being born again into a spiritual kingdom in the present age. The New Covenant will bring about universal righteousness, peace, and prosperity in the new heavens and the new earth only because it first starts by calling out a spiritual people unto a heavenly kingdom in the midst of this fallen world.

Therefore, in this sense, the promises of the Old and New Covenants are the same, but they employ two wholly different ways of seeking to accomplish their end objectives. The Old Covenant, by the works of the law, sought to enter the House of God through the back door (which always remained locked for the sinner). By grace, on the other hand, the New Covenant opens the front door of the House of God for the believer using the key to the finished work of Christ Jesus. For this reason, the New Covenant is superior to the Old Covenant. Unlike the Old Covenant, the grace of the New Covenant has the power to save sinners and usher believers into the presence of God because it begins by effectually changing their hearts.

The Physical Typified the Spiritual

Nevertheless, although God redeems the soul before He redeems the body, God revealed the law of the Old Covenant before He formally established the New Covenant. In other words, even though the spiritual kingdom of this age comes before the creation of the new heavens and the new earth in the age to come, the spiritual kingdom was foreshadowed by the physical kingdom of Israel in the previous age.

In the order of salvation, the spiritual comes before the physical, but in the order of revelation, the physical is revealed before the spiritual.

The Order of Revelation	The Order of Salvation
○ Physical, then Spiritual	○ Spiritual, then Physical
○ The Old Covenant, then the New Covenant	○ New Heart, then Obedience
	○ Grace, then Works
○ Law, then Grace	○ Live, then do this
○ Do this, then Live	○ Redemption of the Soul, then Glorification of the Body
○ Ishmael, then Isaac	
○ Animal Sacrifices, then Christ	○ The Spiritual Kingdom, then the New Earth
○ Israel, then the Church	

Thus, the ineffectual and physical realities of the Old Covenant, which were revealed first, were only shadows and types of the effectual and spiritual realities of the New Covenant, which was established later. "For...the law has but a shadow of the good things to come instead of the true form of these realities" (Heb. 10:1).

The Old Covenant was powerless to fulfill the spiritual promises of the Abrahamic Covenant, and it could not bring even the physical promises to their ultimate fulfillment. The physical seed, land, kingdom, and temple come first and may have looked like the fulfillment of the physical promises, but because of their inability to produce the inward and spiritual promises, they were merely pictures or shadows of the spiritual and physical realities which were to be established afterward by the New Covenant. To put it more plainly, although the Mosaic Covenant promised eternal life, it could not provide eternal life for the sinner, therefore the Mosaic Covenant, at best, was a temporal and typological covenant that pointed to the spiritual and eternal realities that would later be established in the New Covenant.

For this reason, the Old Covenant was a temporal covenant that was not designed to last forever. The ineffectual shadows of the Old Covenant were to continue until the effectual and eternal realities of the New Covenant were established in Christ Jesus, and then they were to pass away.

For instance, the edifice of the Old Covenant, as it were, was built out of earthly materials: wood, stone, and rock. It was established upon a physical mountain, written upon earthly tablets of stone, directed to a physical people, and centered on a temple made by men's hands. The New Covenant, on the other hand, is established upon a spiritual and heavenly foundation and is built by the Holy Spirit out of "living stones" (1 Pet. 2:5). This is what is meant when the author of Hebrews writes, "For you have not come to what may be touched... But you have come to Mount Zion and to the city of the living God, the heavenly Jerusalem...and to Jesus, the mediator of a New Covenant" (Heb. 12:18, 22, 24).

Just as there was an earthly shaking at the inauguration of the Old Covenant at Mount Sinai, there would be another shaking, as the prophet Haggai foretold. "Yet once more I will shake not only the earth but also the heavens" (Heb. 12:26). According to the author of Hebrews, the shaking of the heavens would signify "the removal of things that are shaken—that is, things that have been made—in order that the things that cannot be shaken may remain" (Heb. 12:27). Just as an earthquake brings down buildings made out of earthly materials, this heavenly shaking did away with all of the Old Testament shadows. It brought down everything that is material and temporary and left behind only the things which are spiritual and unmovable. When Christ died, the earth shook and the temple veil was ripped open, exposing the way in to the Holy of Holies once for all (Matt. 27:51).

This is important because the spiritual realities of the New Covenant do not replace the shadows of the Old Covenant. That is, the spiritual seed of Abraham does not replace the physical seed of Abraham. The spiritual kingdom does not replace the geopolitical nation. The Church does not replace Israel. Rather, the spiritual children and the spiritual kingdom are the true fulfillment of the Abrahamic Covenant, for these Old Covenant realities were merely empty shadows of the eternal realities of the New Covenant. For this reason, John Owen stated:

> Abraham, on the account of his faith, and not of his separation according to the flesh, was the father of all that believe, and heir of the world. And in the covenant made with him, as to that which concerns, not the bringing forth of the promised Seed according to the flesh, but as unto faith therein, and in the work of redemption to be performed thereby, lies the foundation of the church in all ages. Wheresoever this covenant is, and with whomsoever it is established, with them is the church; unto whom all the promises and privileges of the church do belong. Hence it was, that at the coming of the Messiah there was not one church taken away, and another set up in the room thereof; but the church continued the same, in those what were the children of Abraham according to the faith. The Christian church is not another church, but the very same that was

before the coming of Christ, having the same faith with it, and interested in the same covenant.[8]

The fact that believing Gentiles are now engrafted into the tree of God's covenantal people, does not mean that Israel has been replaced by the church because, even within the Old Testament dispensation, spiritual Israel never included all of physical Israel (Rom. 9:6-8). Spiritual Israel was limited to the elect of God who were a remnant out of physical Israel. It was the remnant, not Israel as a whole, that God had determined to save, for as it was written, "O LORD, save your people, the remnant of Israel" (Jer. 31:7).

This means that not all members of physical Israel belonged to spiritual Israel, and it also means believing Gentiles do not replace spiritual Israel. Instead, Gentiles, by faith, are united with spiritual Israel by becoming members of it, as Hosea predicted: "Those who were not my people I will call 'my people,' and her who was not beloved I will call 'beloved'" (Rom. 9:25). Within the true Israel of God, there is no difference between believing Jews and believing Gentiles. The middle wall of partition that used to separate them has been broken down in Christ (Eph. 2:11-21). In this way, God's people are one in both dispensations.

The spiritual blessings of the New Covenant were already present in the Old Testament. However, they were clouded over and masked by the earthly and temporal shadows of the Old Covenant. As we have seen, even in the Old Testament period, the true children of Abraham were limited to those circumcised in the heart. The believing remnant was present, but they were hard to see because believers were intermixed with non-believers—who far outnumbered them. Prior to the establishment of the New Covenant, Abraham's children of

---

[8] Owen, *An Exposition of the Epistle to the Hebrews*, 1:123.

faith were not called to separate themselves from the unbelieving children of Abraham.

Believing Jews, as the spiritual children of Abraham, belonged to the Covenant of Grace and were heirs to its promises. They were, nevertheless, externally treated no differently than unbelieving slaves who were required to follow the "weak and worthless elementary principles" of the Old Covenant (Gal. 4:9).

Therefore, the shaking of the New Covenant did not replace Israel with the Church; rather, it removed the dark shadows of the Old Covenant so the spiritual kingdom could be more clearly exposed. The spiritual children of Abraham did not replace the physical children of Abraham any more than Isaac replaced Ishmael. As Ishmael was driven away and forsaken in the desert in order to clarify that Isaac was the heir to the promises, so the physical children of Abraham were officially cut off to reveal that the promises, all along, had belonged solely to the spiritual children of Abraham. The Church (i.e., the spiritual kingdom of God) has been God's redemptive plan from the beginning, for spiritual Israel has always consisted of believers alone in both the Old and New Testaments.

The Promised Kingdom Was Spiritual

The author of Hebrews concluded his explanation of the differences between the types of the Old Covenant and the realities of the New Covenant with these words: "Therefore let us be grateful for receiving a kingdom that cannot be shaken" (Heb. 12:28). The temporal and geopolitical nation of Israel has been removed (not replaced) so the spiritual and eternal kingdom of God can be more clearly seen. The physical kingdom of the Old Testament was only a temporary shadow (that was never intended to last) of the spiritual and eternal kingdom of the New Covenant.

Even Abraham realized the Promised Land was not an earthly inheritance to be received this side of the resurrection. Throughout Abraham's earthly life, he never inherited any of the land. By faith, Abraham was not even looking to inherit any land this side of glory (Heb. 11:10). In addition, Joshua, the military captain who led Israel into the Promised Land, did not believe Canaan was the eternal possession promised to Abraham. "For if Joshua had given them rest, God would not have spoken of another day later on" (Heb. 4:8). In regard to this, the author of Hebrews writes:

> These all died in faith, not having received the things promised, but having seen them and greeted them from afar, and having acknowledged that they were strangers and exiles on the earth. For people who speak thus make it clear that they are seeking a homeland. If they had been thinking of that land from which they had gone out, they would have had opportunity to return. But as it is, they desire a better country, that is, a heavenly one. Therefore God is not ashamed to be called their God, for he has prepared for them a city (Heb. 11:13-16).

From the beginning, the kingdom promised to Abraham was spiritual and heavenly in nature, and, by faith, Abraham and Joshua understood this. The citizens of the kingdom of God would consist of only those who were born again and declared righteous in Christ (Jn. 3:3). Jesus refused to have anything to do with sitting upon a geopolitical throne to rule over the wicked and unbelieving physical seed of Abraham (Jn. 6:15). Rather, He declared, "My kingdom is not of this world. If my kingdom were of this world, my servants would have been fighting, that I might not be delivered over to the Jews. But my kingdom is not from the world" (Jn. 18:36). In another place, Christ explained, "The kingdom of God is not coming in ways that can be observed, nor will they say, 'Look, here it is!' or 'There!' for behold, the kingdom of God is in the midst of you" (Lk. 17:20-21). Paul likewise said, "flesh and blood cannot inherit the kingdom of God" (1 Cor. 15:50).

In this age, the principal concern of the kingdom of God, according to Anthony Hoekema, is not for the Lord to overcome the political foes of Israel, but to overcome the power of sin and usher in the eternal age of righteousness.[9] For instance, in every soul that is born from above, in every temptation that is resisted by the power of the Spirit, and in every place where Christ is proclaimed and received by faith, a glimpse of the kingdom of God is seen shining forth its present power over sin. Herman Ridderbos rightly tied the coming of the kingdom of God to the gospel of Jesus Christ: "The secret of the kingdom of heaven lies in Jesus' victory over Satan, in his unlimited miraculous power, his unrestricted authority to preach the gospel, in his pronounce-ments of blessedness and the bestowal of salvation upon his people."[10]

And Louis Berkhof summarized the kingdom of God with these words:

> The Kingdom of God is primarily an eschatological concept. The fundamental idea of the Kingdom in Scripture is not that of a restored theocratic kingdom of God in Christ – which is essentially a kingdom of Israel–, as the Premillenarians claim; neither is it a new social condition, pervaded by the Spirit of Christ, and realized by man through such external means as good laws, civilization, education, social reforms, and so on, as the Modernists

---

[9] See Anthony Hoekema, *The Bible and the Future* (Grand Rapids: Eerdmans, 1994), 45.

[10] Herman Ridderbos, *The Coming of the Kingdom* (Philadelphia, PA: P&R, 1962), 82.

would have us believe. The primary idea of the Kingdom of God in Scripture is that of the rule of God established and acknowledged in the hearts of sinners by the powerful regenerating influence of the Holy Spirit, insuring them of the inestimable blessings of salvation, – a rule that is realized in principle on earth, but will not reach its culmination until the visible and glorious return of Jesus Christ.[11]

Yes, the physical promises of the Abrahamic Covenant will be fulfilled in the age to come, but not until all the spiritual realities are dealt with first in the present age. Consequently, the kingdom of God will not be completely consummated until the last enemy (i.e., death) is destroyed (1 Cor. 15:20-28). After death has been destroyed in the general resurrection of the dead, Christ will establish the new heavens and the new earth—an eternal kingdom where only righteousness dwells forever (2 Pet. 3:13). "At last," Charles Alexander proclaimed, "the drama of creation is worked out to its magnificent conclusion and all heaven bursts into praise and admiration at the victorious result of all the travail entered into by the Godhead. There will never be another challenge to the divine will for the voices in heaven declare, 'And He shall reign forever and ever.'"[12]

Conclusion

The last three chapters have highlighted the dual fulfillment of the Abrahamic Covenant. We have seen how the Old Testament focuses upon the physical, typological, and ineffectual fulfillment, while the New Testament focuses upon the supernatural and effectual fulfillment of the Abrahamic

---

[11] Louis Berkhof, *Systematic Theology* (Grand Rapids: Eerdmans, 1994), 568.

[12] Charles D. Alexander, *Revelation Spiritually Understood*, April 20, 2013, available at: http://www.allbygrace.com/alexrev047-14.html

Covenant. Having observed these two separate fulfillments, we will go on to survey some additional biblical support for the dual nature of the Abrahamic Covenant. In all this, we have concluded that the conditions placed upon the physical seed of Abraham were fulfilled in Christ Jesus which brought about the unconditional promise God made to Abraham. By faith alone, these blessings are enjoyed by God's true people who consist of believers alone throughout the history of redemption.

6

New Testament Affirmation

The dichotomous nature of the Abrahamic Covenant is not gleaned only from the wording of the Abrahamic Covenant (Gen. 17:4-14). It is also clearly affirmed in the New Testament. In fact, the apostle Paul, the quintessential covenant theologian, had a lot to say about the relationship between the Old and New Testaments. Therefore, to further understand the nature of the Abrahamic Covenant, we now turn to the writings of Paul. As we shall discover in these next two chapters, Paul understood and taught the dichotomous nature of the Abrahamic Covenant.

The Two Covenants of Abraham (Galatians 4:22-31)

In Galatians 4:22-31, Paul gave a quick and concise overview of his inspired view of the Abrahamic Covenant. He succinctly explained the allegorical differences between Abraham's two sons (Ishmael and Isaac), and their analogous relationships to the two separate covenants that find their roots in Abraham. According to Paul, the first covenant was conditional and led to bondage, and the second covenant was unconditional and leads to freedom. The first covenant proceeding from Abraham was ultimately the Mosaic Covenant of Works delivered at Mount Sinai. The second covenant proceeding from Abraham is the ultimately the New Covenant of Grace.

The Allegory Presented

Paul began his allegory by claiming that Abraham's two wives, Sarah and Hagar, represent two different covenants:

> For it is written that Abraham had two sons, one by a slave woman and one by a free woman. But the son of the slave was born according to the flesh, while the son of the free woman was born through promise. Now this may be interpreted allegorically: these women are two covenants (Gal. 4:22-24a).

Paul demonstrated the typical nature of Abraham's two sons by showing that their mothers and the nature of their births were symbolic as well. Ishmael, the nature of his birth, and Hagar represent the Covenant of Works. Isaac, the nature of his birth, and Sarah represent the covenant of promise and grace.

According to Paul, the main difference between these two children was their mothers. Importantly, it was their respective mothers that determined which of the sons received the promised inheritance. Being born of a slave or free woman determined that the child himself would be born into slavery or freedom.

Hagar:
The Conditional Dimension of the Abrahamic Covenant

According to Paul, Hagar, the mother of Ishmael, represented the conditional covenant made with Abraham. Ishmael's mother and the nature of Ishmael's birth depicted a conditional covenant that leads to bondage. Just as Ishmael was born from Hagar, the slave woman, so it is for all those who are born into the Covenant of Works. Ishmael was born under the law and in slavery to the dominion of sin, as are all those who are born after the flesh (Rom. 6).

Ishmael also represents the Covenant of Works because there was nothing supernatural about the nature of his birth. Ishmael's birth required no faith on Abraham's part, and therefore, he was not the child of promise. Similarly, just as Ishmael was not the promised "seed," so it is with all Abraham's physical children who are not born again by the Spirit, for there is nothing supernatural or spiritual for those born after the flesh. "That which is born of the flesh is flesh, and that which is born of the Spirit is spirit" (Jn. 3:6). "This means that it is not the children of the flesh who are the children of God..." (Rom. 9:8).

Sarah:
The Unconditional Dimension of the Abrahamic Covenant

The details of Isaac's birth were the opposite of Ishmael's. Isaac's mother represented the unconditional covenant of grace revealed to Abraham. Isaac was born (1) supernaturally, (2) by the free woman, and (3) according to the promise. In a sense, these characteristics are true of all those who have been born again by the Spirit into the Covenant of Grace.

In the verses above (Gal. 4:22-24), Paul focused upon the differences between the births of these two children. Although both were the physical children of Abraham and circumcised in the flesh, only one was the child of promise. This, being allegorical, shows the great difference between the Covenant of Works and the Covenant of Grace. Those who are born into the Covenant of Works are born slaves, while those who are born into the Covenant of Grace are born free.

The Allegory Explained

The important thing to note, according to Paul, is that these two mothers were representative of "two covenants" (Gal. 4:24). Paul went on to explain how these different mothers (Hagar and Sarah) represented the difference between the physical seed and spiritual seed of Abraham. In so doing, Paul linked the physical seed with the Covenant of Works and the spiritual seed with the Covenant of Grace.

> Now this may be interpreted allegorically: these women are two covenants. One is from Mount Sinai, bearing children for slavery; she is Hagar. Now Hagar is Mount Sinai in Arabia; she corresponds to the present Jerusalem, for she is in slavery with her children. But the Jerusalem above is free, and she is our mother. For it is written, "Rejoice, O barren one who does not bear; break forth and cry aloud, you who are not in labor! For the children of the desolate one will be more than those of the one who has a husband." Now you, brothers, like Isaac, are children of promise (Gal. 4:24-28).

The Slave Woman Represents the Old Covenant

Hagar, the Arabian bondwoman, represents the physical seed of Abraham and the Mosaic Covenant of Works, for "she is in slavery with her children." Hagar shows that the physical children of Abraham, those who were "born according to the flesh," were born into bondage under the dominion of sin. The historical covenant established with Abraham's physical seed was the Mosaic Covenant, and Paul linked the Mosaic Covenant with Hagar and her son when he stated, "One is from Mount Sinai, bearing children for slavery; she is Hagar. Now Hagar is Mount Sinai in Arabia" (Gal. 4:24-25).

The Lord told the Jews, that despite their Abrahamic heritage, they were born in slavery to sin (Jn. 8:34-38). Thus,

Paul concluded that unbelieving Jews were not any better off than the unbelieving Gentiles: "What then? Are we Jews any better off? No, not at all. For we have already charged that all, both Jews and Greeks, are under sin" (Rom. 3:9).

The Free Woman Represents the New Covenant

In contrast, Sarah represents the New Covenant. Sarah, unlike Hagar, was a free woman and the mother of the child of promise. Sarah represents "the Jerusalem above" which is also free. Just as the slave woman represents the Mosaic Covenant of bondage, the free woman represents the New Covenant of freedom.

Just as Isaac was born free as the supernatural child of promise, so are the spiritual children of Abraham born free by their supernatural birth. This agrees with what Paul said earlier in Galatians: "And if you are Christ's, then you are Abraham's offspring, heirs according to promise" (Gal. 3:29).

The Allegory Applied

Just as Abraham had two sons that were born from two different women, Abraham had two seeds that were born from two different covenants (the Old and New Covenants), and the two seeds are his physical and spiritual children. This dual covenantal framework is in harmony with Paul's application and conclusion:

> But just as at that time he who was born according to the flesh persecuted him who was born according to the Spirit, so also it is now. But what does the Scripture say? "Cast out the slave woman and her son, for the son of the slave woman shall not inherit with the son of the free woman." So, brothers, we are not children of the slave but of the free woman (Gal. 4:29-31).

The Physical Seed and the Covenant of Works

The Apostle Paul had a deep love for his own kinsmen. He was not ashamed of being a Jew, and he realized the Jewish people were born privileged. Yet Paul also knew being born from Jewish parents alone did not bring a child into the covenant of grace. Paul understood "that it is not the children of the flesh who are the children of God, but the children of the promise are counted as offspring" (Rom. 9:8). Paul knew even Jews had to be born again by the Spirit.

As a race of people, Paul placed the physical children of Abraham in the same category as the Ishmaelites. According to Jonathan Edwards, "They were rejected and cast off from being any longer God's visible people. They were broken off from the stock of Abraham, and since then have no more been reputed his seed than the Ishmaelites or Edomites, who are as much his natural seed as they."[1]

Ishmael was Abraham's physical seed, but he was not the child of promise. Because of this, after Isaac was born, Ishmael and his mother, Hagar, were driven out into the wilderness, for it is written: "Cast out the slave woman and her son, for the son of the slave woman shall not inherit with the son of the free woman" (Gal. 4:30).

Although this was historically true for Ishmael, when Paul said, "The son of the slave woman shall not be heir with the son of the free woman," he was not referring to Ishmael or the Ishmaelites. Rather, he was referring to the Israelites, "the present Jerusalem." Just as Ishmael was not the seed God had in mind when He promised Abraham a son, the physical

---

[1] Jonathan Edwards, *A History of the Work of Redemption* (Edinburgh: Banner of Truth Trust, 2003), 297.

children of Abraham were never intended to be the children of promise (Rom. 9:8).

God commanded Abraham to drive Hagar and his own physical son Ishmael away into the wilderness, so Abraham deserted the Arabian bondwoman and her child, driving them out into the desert sands. In the same way, God has deserted the House of Israel: "See, your house is left to you desolate" (Matt. 23:38).

The Mosaic Covenant was established in the desert, and its members, because they were the children of bondage, were ultimately deserted there as well. This may sound harsh, but without the righteousness of Christ, no one will see God. Similarly, just as the full inheritance went to Isaac and not Ishmael, the kingdom promised to Abraham has been given solely to the spiritual seed of Abraham while the unbelieving physical seed of Abraham have been completely cut off from the promised inheritance (Matt. 21:43).

Paul explained that, for the same reason the Ishmaelites persecuted the Israelites, now the Israelites are persecuting the church: "But just as at that time he who was born according to the flesh persecuted him who was born according to the Spirit, so also it is now" (Gal. 4:29). Just as Ishmael had no inheritance with Isaac, the nation of Israel has no spiritual inheritance with those who have been quickened together with Christ.

The Spiritual Seed and the Covenant of Grace

Abraham's physical children, because they were born by the works of the flesh, are the children of bondage. They are not the children of promise, for there was nothing supernatural about their birth.

On the other hand, the spiritual seed of Abraham are the true fulfillment of the Abrahamic Covenant: "Now you, brothers, like Isaac, are children of promise" (Gal. 4:28). "And if you are Christ's, then you are Abraham's offspring, heirs according to promise" (Gal. 3:29). "So, brothers, we are not children of the slave but of the free woman" (Gal. 4:31). The Jerusalem from above is the mother of Abraham's spiritual seed, for believers have not come to Mount Sinai but to Mount Zion. They have come "to the city of the living God, the heavenly Jerusalem, and to innumerable angels in festal gathering, and to the assembly of the firstborn who are enrolled in heaven..." (Heb. 12:22-23).

Michael Horton concludes:

> Personal obedience to commands is a radically different basis for an inheritance than faith in a promise. While the Scriptures uphold the moral law as the abiding way of life for God's redeemed people, it can never be a way to life. Every covenant has two parties, and we assume the responsibilities of faithful partners, but the basis of acceptance with God is the covenant-keeping of another, the Servant of the Lord: and because of his faithfulness, we now inherit all of the promises through faith alone, as children of Sarah and citizens of the heavenly Jerusalem.[2]

Conclusion

Both the Presbyterian and Dispensationalist views of covenantal history hang on to the importance of the physical seed of Abraham. Dispensationalists believe the Jews are still God's covenantal people, while Presbyterians believe their physical children are born into the Covenant of Grace. Yet according to Paul, the physical seed of Abraham were not naturally born

---

[2] Horton, *God of Promise*, 76.

into the Covenant of Grace. Instead, Abraham's physical seed were born into the Covenant of Works. This means the true children of promise are only those who have been supernaturally born again by the Spirit of God. In other words, the promised children of Abraham are those who have the faith of Abraham.

7

The Dual Covenantal Framework of Romans

The apostle Paul did not encourage the children of Abraham to look to their covenantal standing before God, for he knew the physical seed of Abraham, including himself, needed rescuing from their covenantal standing. This was because the Jews were not born into the Covenant of Grace, but, like the Gentiles, they were born as sinners into the Covenant of Works. Although the Jews were given the gospel in the Abrahamic Covenant, they were placed under the legal obligation to obey God by circumcision of the Abrahamic Covenant and the law of the Mosaic Covenant And because the Jews were born sinners, their covenant obligation did not secure their freedom, but their condemnation.

Therefore, Paul urged the Jews to look away from their covenantal standing and follow the example of Abraham who looked to Christ in faith. Paul exhorted them to reject any pride and confidence they had in their Jewish identity and to seek the righteousness that comes by faith alone. According to Paul, what was important for them was not to find their identity in Abraham but rather to find their identity in Christ alone (Phil. 3:4-10).

That the physical children of Abraham were born under the Covenant of Works is a foundational tenet of Paul's covenantal theology. Paul not only sought to explain this in his epistle to the Galatians, but also in his letter to the Romans.

Although the book of Romans systematically presents the doctrine of salvation, the golden thread that ties the various parts of the book together is Paul's covenantal position. A central concern of the book deals with the covenantal status of the physical children of Abraham. Paul was fully aware that Jewish history dominated the storyline of the Old Testament. Because the gospel had moved away from the Jews to the Gentiles, Paul wanted to explain the current role of the Jewish people in the New Covenant.

Therefore, as Paul systematically unpacked the doctrine of salvation, he related each section to the current state of the Jewish people. In the process, Paul concluded that Abraham had two types of children—physical and spiritual. The Jews were certainly born privileged, but they were also born condemned. The physical children of Abraham were born under the Covenant of Works, while only the spiritual children of Abraham were counted righteous in Christ by faith. Yet Paul provided hope for the Jewish people. Ironically, the Jews could be saved by following the example of the Gentiles who displayed the faith of the Jews' own father, Abraham.

This covenantal framework of Paul verifies the dichotomous nature of the Abrahamic Covenant. The unconditional promise given to Abraham placed his physical children under the legal obligation to obey God. The only hope for the Jewish people, then, was for them to place their faith in the one Seed who fulfilled the promise by keeping the legal obligation of the Covenant of Works—their promised Messiah.

Unfortunately, the Jews gloated in three basic things: (1) the fact that God gave them the law, (2) their circumcision, which separated them from the rest of the ungodly nations, and (3) their father Abraham. These things were of paramount importance in the minds of the Jewish people because they spoke of their distinct Jewish identity and repeatedly pointed to the fact that they had a special covenantal relationship with God.

Therefore, when the gospel broke through to the Gentiles, many of the believing Jews were taken by surprise. Some of them, due to their racial prejudice, even resisted. When the leaders of the church became convinced that Gentiles would be included in the gospel community, a sect spung up that insisted the Gentiles, at the very least, would have to identify themselves with the Jewish people via circumcision. In other words, if Gentiles were going to be included, they would have to become Jewish proselytes. God's people were the Jews, so if Gentiles desired to be a part of the people of God, they would have to join the ranks of the Jewish community by being circumcised because, according to the circumcision sect, there was no salvation outside of physical Israel.

Paul wrote his letter to the churches of Galatia to challenge and disprove this false notion. He explained that faith alone was sufficient to establish a Gentile as a spiritual child of Abraham. Being Jewish had no inherent salvific value. Not only were the Gentiles not required to be circumcised to be among God's people, but also the Jews were required to abandon any trust that they had in their circumcision and their nationality if they wanted to be saved.

Likewise, in his letter to the Romans, Paul sought to explain that the external identifying marks of Jewish ethnic identity had no bearing upon who was, or was not, a part of God's redeemed people. Possession of the law, outward circumcision, and Jewish ethnicity did not equate to a special relationship with God in the Old Testament, nor does it now. Faith alone has always been the only way to have peace with God for both the Jews and the Gentiles throughout redemptive history.

No Racial Partiality with God

Paul began his letter to the Romans by declaring the racial impartiality of God (2:11). It is important to remember that the racial separation in the Old Testament helped preserve the genealogical line of Christ. This wall of division between Jews and Gentiles was very important, for salvation (Christ) would be from the Jews. Yet now that the promise of the Abrahamic Covenant has been fulfilled in Christ, the dividing wall between Jews and Gentiles has been broken down (Eph. 2:14). The Jews no longer have exclusive rights to the gospel. According to Paul, the gospel is impartial and has gone into all the world and is powerful enough to save both Jews and Gentiles: "For I am not ashamed of the gospel, for it is the power of God for salvation to everyone who believes, to the Jew first and also to the Greek" (Rom. 1:16).

Not only is the gospel impartial, but the law also is impartial: "There will be tribulation and distress for every human being who does evil, the Jew first and the Greek, but glory and honor and peace for everyone who does good, the Jew first and also the Greek. For God shows no partiality" (Rom. 2:9-11).

The law and the gospel do not show any racial favoritism. Gentiles can be saved by the gospel, just as Jews can be condemned by the law: "For all who have sinned without the law will also perish without the law, and all who have sinned under the law will be judged by the law" (Rom. 2:12).

The Jews Should Not Trust in Their Possession of the Law

After declaring the racial impartiality of God, Paul went on to attack the pride that the Jews had in their possession of the law of God. Of all the people groups of the world, God chose to reveal His law to the Israelites. No doubt, this was a blessing, but it was also a stumbling block for the Jews. The law was given to show them their sins and point them to their future Messiah, but the Jews sought to use the law to establish their own righteousness.

The Jews seemed to think their possession and knowledge of the law gave them some special relationship with God: "You call yourself a Jew and rely on the law and boast in God and know his will and approve what is excellent, because you are instructed from the law" (Rom. 2:17-18). However, Paul confronted this false notion with these words:

> For all who have sinned without the law will also perish without the law, and all who have sinned under the law will be judged by the law. For it is not the hearers of the law who are righteous before God, but the doers of the law who will be justified. For when Gentiles, who do not have the law, by nature do what the law requires, they are a law to themselves, even though they do not have the law (Rom. 2:12-14).

Paul corrected this prideful notion of the Jews by explaining that they were not the only ones who possessed the law. The Jews could not boast in the fact that they had the law (written upon tablets of stone) when the Gentiles also had the law (written upon their consciences). Additionally, possession of the law is of no value unless you can keep the law. Since the Jews could not keep the law, they were just as condemned by the law as were the Gentiles. Thus, Gentiles are condemned by the law that is written upon their consciences, while Jews are condemned by the law that was given to them by Moses. Concerning the law, the Jews had no special boasting rights before God.

The Jews Should Not Trust in Their Circumcision

The second thing the Jews boasted in was their circumcision, the identifying mark that separated them from the pagans who had no knowledge of God. Paul rebuked this false notion of superiority:

> For circumcision indeed is of value if you obey the law, but if you break the law, your circumcision becomes uncircumcision. So, if a man who is uncircumcised keeps the precepts of the law, will not his uncircumcision be regarded as circumcision? Then he who is physically uncircumcised but keeps the law will condemn you who have the written code and circumcision but break the law (Rom. 2:25-27).

The Jews Should Not Trust in Their Ethnicity

The third thing that the Jews needed to abandon was their confidence in their Jewish ethnicity. Paul transitioned from the subject of circumcision to the Jewish race which was identified by circumcision: "For no one is a Jew who is merely one outwardly, nor is circumcision outward and physical. But a Jew is one inwardly, and circumcision is a matter of the heart, by the Spirit, not by the letter. His praise is not from man but from God" (Rom. 2:28-29). In other words, being a circumcised Jew did not make a person a spiritual child of Abraham. The Jews could boast in their circumcision, but only the spiritually circumcised could boast in God. That is, a real Jew is a person who has been born from above by the Holy Spirit.

Is There Any Advantage in Being Jewish?

The Jews assumed they had a special relationship with God because of their law, circumcision, and bloodline. In the first two chapters of Romans, Paul systematically pulled out all these false supports from underneath the Jews. In the process of seeking to humble the Jews, Paul placed them in the same covenantal category as the Gentiles - condemned by God under the Covenant of Works. He then anticipated the Jewish response when he went on to state: "Then what advantage has the Jew? Or what is the value of circumcision?" (Rom. 3:1). If Jews are not automatically born into a righteous standing with God, and if Jews and Gentiles are both under the same legal condemnation, then what advantage do the Jews have?

Early Access to the Gospel

Paul answered this question in the positive: "Much in every way. To begin with, the Jews were entrusted with the oracles of God" (Rom. 3:2). The Jews had a huge advantage. Chiefly, the Jews had early access to the knowledge of the gospel. Not only was the gospel revealed to the Jews in the unconditional side of the Abrahamic Covenant, but also the Mosaic Covenant itself bore witness to the gospel. "But now the righteousness of God has been manifested apart from the law, although the Law and the Prophets bear witness to it - the righteousness of God through faith in Jesus Christ for all who believe" (Rom. 3:21- 22).

However, to make sure his readers did not confuse the Law of Moses with the gospel of Christ, Paul reminded them that the gospel, which reveals the imputed righteousness of Christ, was manifested independently of the Mosaic Covenant. That is, the Mosaic Covenant did not establish for its membership the righteousness that is received by faith in the gospel.[1]

Nevertheless, although the Mosaic Covenant was not the gospel, it bore witness to the gospel. As Douglas Moo states: "While God's justifying activity in the new age takes part outside the confines of the Old Covenant, the OT as a whole anticipates and predicts this new work of God: God's righteousness is witnessed to by the law and the prophets."[2] In other words, although the Old Covenant did not establish the gospel, it expected, predicted, and pointed to the gospel.

This means that for thousands of years the Jews had the witness of the gospel while Gentiles were left in darkness. Although the Mosaic Covenant condemned them, they could, at any time, have been saved, by looking to the promised Messiah in faith. This was the advantage the Jews had over the Gentiles, and what an advantage it was!

In this way, the Jews have a rich heritage, and, historically, they have been given a leg up on the Gentiles. Similarly, although Baptists do not believe their children are automatically born into the Covenant of Grace, this should not be taken to imply their children are not born into privilege. A Christian home is a huge advantage. Prayer and faithful biblical instruction in law and gospel are the normal means of

---

[1] Douglas Moo provides a good explanation of this: "In the new era inaugurated by Christ's death God has acted to deliver and vindicate his people 'apart from' the law. It is not primarily the law as something for humans to do, but the law system, as a stage in God's unfolding plan, that is in view here. 'Law' (nomos), then, refers to the 'Mosaic Covenant,' that (temporary) administration set up between God and his people to regulate their lives and reveal their sin until the establishment of the promise in Christ" ("The Epistle to the Romans," in *New International Commentary on the New Testament*. Grand Rapids: Eerdmans, 1996, 223).

[2] Moo, "*The Epistle to the Romans*, 223.

grace that God has chosen to utilize to call His people to Himself. Clearly, however, just because the Jews and the children of Christian parents have knowledge of the gospel does not mean that they are automatic partakers of the gospel.

No Present Advantages

If the Jews' previous advantage was their access to the gospel, what advantage do they have now that the gospel has been commissioned to go to the Gentiles? The apostle Paul deals with this question: "What then? Are we Jews any better off? No, not at all. For we have already charged that all, both Jews and Greeks, are under sin" (Rom. 3:9). Thus, Paul concluded that the Jews have no current advantages over the Gentiles.

Herman Witsius wrote concerning this, "Yet, none of these things [the law, circumcision, and bloodline], nay not all of them put together, if we only consider the external confederation, was sufficient to them for salvation; for 'they are not all Israel, which are of Israel; neither because they are the seed of Abraham, are they all children.'"[3] Nehemiah Coxe understood this as well: "The Jew had a great advantage and there was profit in circumcision...And yet all this lies short of an actual, personal, and saving interest in the Covenant of Grace."[4] Herman Ridderbos also concluded:

> And insofar as [historical Israel] rejects Christ promises given to Abraham and his seed. And insofar as it rejects Christ and trusts in the possession of the law, circumcision and its own righteousness, it can no longer assert its right to

---

[3] Herman Witsius, *The Economy of the Divine Covenants between God and Man* (Phillipsburg, NJ: P&R, 1990), IV. XI. IV.
[4] Coxe and Owen, *Covenant Theology*, 114.

the name and privilege of Israel in the redemptive-historical sense.[5]

Paul excluded any boasting rights for the Jewish people:

> Then what becomes of our boasting? It is excluded. By what kind of law? By a law of works? No, but by the law of faith. For we hold that one is justified by faith apart from works of the law. Or is God the God of Jews only? Is he not the God of Gentiles also? Yes, of Gentiles also, since God is one – who will justify the circumcised by faith and the uncircumcised through faith (Rom. 3:27-30).

Interestingly, both Dispensationalists and covenantal Presbyterians believe Abraham's physical seed are born into some special relationship with God that sets them above the unbelieving Gentiles. But Paul clearly removed any of these outward advantages and placed the unbelieving Jews in the same camp as the unbelieving Gentiles.

Thus, while covenantal Baptists are grateful that their children are born surrounded by the law and the gospel, all these outward advantages are of no avail unless there is death to the law and saving faith in the gospel. Although we sincerely desire the salvation of the Jewish people, they will perish without inheriting the blessings of Abraham unless they repent and believe the same gospel that has now been given to the Gentiles.

The Unique Place of Abraham

If the unbelieving Jews are no better off than the unbelieving Gentiles, then what about Abraham? Surely, Abraham was special. Did not God choose Abraham, and were not the Jews Abraham's seed? If the Jews are not special, then this must

---

[5] Herman Ridderbos, *Paul: An Outline of His Theology* (Grand Rapids: Eerdmans, 1975), 354.

mean Abraham and his circumcision were not special. Anticipating this rebuttal, Paul stated,

> What then shall we say was gained by Abraham, our forefather according to the flesh? For if Abraham was justified by works, he has something to boast about, but not before God. For what does the Scripture say? "Abraham believed God, and it was counted to him as righteousness" (Rom. 4:1-3).

That is to say that there was nothing physically, genetically, or ethically special about Abraham. What made Abraham special was not his circumcision, his parentage, or his obedience to the law—but his faith.

The Purpose of Abraham's Circumcision

If this was the case, then why was Abraham circumcised? If being Jewish means nothing and circumcision means nothing, then why was the Father of the Jews circumcised? Were the Jews not following Abraham's example in their own circumcision?

By anticipating this objection, Paul went on to explain that Abraham was circumcised because he was a believer, and not because he was born into the right family. This is important because Abraham's circumcision, unlike infant circumcision, was a sign and seal of the righteousness that is imputed by faith: "He received the sign of circumcision as a seal of the righteousness that he had by faith while he was still uncircumcised" (Rom. 4:11a).

For Paul, the chronological order of Abraham's faith, justification, and circumcision was a very important detail. Abraham's circumcision showed how he could be the father of all believers (i.e., his spiritual seed): "The purpose was to make him the father of all who believe without being circumcised, so that righteousness would be counted to them as well" (Rom. 4:11b). As Robert Haldane explained: Abraham's circumcision "was appointed as a figure or sign of his paternity, literally with respect to a numerous seed, and spiritually of all believers."[6] Thus, the timing of Abraham's circumcision showed how his spiritual seed could be declared righteous apart from being circumcised in the flesh.

Abraham's circumcision is unique, differing from the circumcision of his infant male children. Even though Abraham's physical seed were required to be circumcised (Gen. 17:14),[7] following the example of Abraham, the spiritual seed are not under such an obligation. Those who believe are justified by faith alone, independent of circumcision.

When Paedobaptists use Romans 4:11 as a proof text to support infant baptism, they do so without properly separating believer's circumcision from infant circumcision. Although Abraham's circumcision signified his justification by faith alone, it did not mean infant circumcision held such significance.

In fact, connecting Abraham's circumcision with infant circumcision reverses Paul's argument. Paul explained how believing Gentiles could be brought into the Covenant of Grace without circumcision, not how Abraham's unbelieving physical children could be brought in the Covenant of Grace without faith. The point that Paul was making is that the physical seed of Abraham cannot look to Abraham's circumcision as grounds to boast in their own circumcision.

---

[6] Robert Haldane, *Romans* (Edinburgh: Banner of Truth Trust, 1996), 174.
[7] This was a protective measure to help ensure the ethnic purity of the line of the Messiah.

The Inheritance of Abraham Is by Faith Alone

After four chapters, Paul had dismantled every reason for the Jews to think they were special before God. The Jews cannot boast in their circumcision, in their possession of the law, in their father Abraham, or even in the circumcision of Abraham. All these things are of no avail to them.

Paul concluded his argument by claiming that the full inheritance of Abraham is received by faith alone and by Abraham's spiritual seed alone:

> For the promise to Abraham and his offspring that he would be heir of the world did not come through the law but through the righteousness of faith. For if it is the adherents of the law who are to be the heirs, faith is null and the promise is void. For the law brings wrath, but where there is no law there is no transgression. That is why it depends on faith, in order that the promise may rest on grace and be guaranteed to all his offspring – not only to the adherent of the law but also to the one who shares the faith of Abraham, who is the father of us all, as it is written, "I have made you the father of many nations" – in the presence of the God in whom he believed, who gives life to the dead and calls into existence the things that do not exist. In hope he believed against hope, that he should become the father of many nations, as he had been told, "So shall your offspring be." [...] That is why his faith was "counted to him as righteousness." But the words "it was counted to him" were not written for his sake alone, but for ours also. It will be counted to us who believe in him who raised from the dead Jesus our Lord (Rom. 4:13-18, 22-24).

Why Were Gentiles Outnumbering the Jews?

However, a question remains. If the promised inheritance is received by faith alone, and if these promises were given to

Abraham and to his descendants, why were the Jews excluded from their inheritance? Why were the Jews rejecting the promises in unbelief? By contrast, the Gentiles were rushing into the promised kingdom, by faith, with greater ease than the Jews. Why was this? Why were the Gentiles, who were not expecting any inheritance, flooding into the kingdom? More importantly, why were the Jews, who were eagerly awaiting the kingdom, stubbornly rejecting it once it arrived?

If incorporating the Gentiles into the covenant blessings was not difficult enough for the Jews to accept, it had to have been even more difficult for them to know that Gentile converts were outnumbering Jewish converts.

It was one thing for Gentiles to be brought into the promised inheritance but quite another thing for the uncircumcised Gentiles to be outnumbering the Jews. If things continued, the kingdom would soon lose its Jewish identity all together. Why were so many Jews being left out of the kingdom? How could this be?

Before Paul explained why so many Jews were not included in the inheritance, he began by making sure that his readers understood that he was not anti-Semitic: "I am speaking the truth in Christ – I am not lying; my conscience bears me witness in the Holy Spirit – that I have great sorrow and unceasing anguish in my heart. For I could wish that I myself were accursed and cut off from Christ for the sake of my brothers, my kinsmen according to the flesh" (Rom. 9:1-3).

Not only did Paul love the Jewish people, but he also acknowledged that they were given many outward blessings: "They are Israelites, and to them belong the adoption, the glory, the covenants, the giving of the law, the worship, and the promises. To them belong the patriarchs, and from their race, according to the flesh, is the Christ, who is God over all, blessed forever. Amen" (Rom. 9:4-5).

These outward advantages were what made it seem so strange for the Gentiles to be entering into the kingdom with greater ease than the Jews. The Gentiles had always been at a disadvantage. Prior to the cross, Gentiles were "alienated from the commonwealth of Israel and strangers to the covenants of promise, having no hope and without God in the world" (Eph. 2:12). Yet after the cross, the Gentiles were coming into the kingdom in droves.

After reminding the Jews of his love for them and acknowledging that they, rather than the Gentiles, were originally given the promises, Paul explained why the Jews were rejecting the promises and why the Gentiles were embracing them by faith.

Not All Israel Is of Israel

But first Paul removed any misplaced charge against God: "But it is not as though the word of God has failed" (Rom. 9:6). Just because most of the Jews were not inheriting the kingdom did not mean God was unfaithful in keeping his promise to Abraham. Why? Because even though the inheritance was promised to Israel, it was not physical Israel that God had in mind: "For not all who are descended from Israel belong to Israel, and not all are children of Abraham because they are his offspring, but 'Through Isaac shall your offspring be named'" (Rom. 9:6-7). The inheritance was never intended for all of Abraham's physical offspring; rather, it was intended for all his spiritual offspring. This is why Paul said, "This means that it is not the children of the flesh who are the children of God, but the children of the promise are counted as offspring" (Rom. 9:8).

Consequently, the inheritance belonged exclusively to spiritual Israel, which left out many of the Jewish people. Moreover, this was not something new to the New Covenant. It was true throughout redemptive history. It is not as if God had changed His mind about who were to receive the promised inheritance. From the beginning, the inheritance was reserved for only a select few who had been chosen by God. To illustrate this, Paul turned to the story of Jacob and Esau, the twin sons of Isaac, who were both the natural-born, circumcised grandchildren of Abraham. Yet according to Paul, the inheritance was not intended for all of Abraham's physical seed. Rather, it was intended only for those whom God had chosen beforehand:

> For this is what the promise said: "About this time next year I will return, and Sarah shall have a son." And not only so, but also when Rebekah had conceived children by one man, our forefather Isaac, though they were not yet born and had done nothing either good or bad – in order that God's purpose of election might continue, not because of works but because of him who calls—she was told, "The older will serve the younger." As it is written, "Jacob I loved, but Esau I hated" (Rom. 9:9-13).

What made Jacob different from Esau was not his birthright or his works, but divine election. Prior to the birth of these twin boys, there was a prophecy that proclaimed, "The older shall serve the younger" (Gen. 25:23). This prophecy proved that God is the One who determines who will receive the inheritance.

In the same way, prior to the gospel breaking through to the Gentiles, there was an Old Testament prophecy that predicted this event: "Those who were not my people I will call 'my people,' and her who was not beloved I will call 'beloved'" (Rom. 9:25; cf. Hos. 2:23). "And in the place where it was said to them, 'You are not my people,' it shall be said to them, 'Children of the living God'" (Hos. 1:10). In addition, Paul went on to explain that the Old Testament made it clear that only a small number of the physical seed of Abraham would be saved: "And Isaiah cries out concerning Israel: 'Though the number of the sons of Israel be as the sand of the sea, only a remnant of them will be saved'" (Rom. 9:27). Thus, the first reason why the majority of physical Israel were rejecting the kingdom was that the promises were exclusively given to God's elect people, who consisted of Abraham's spiritual seed.

Israel Stumbled Over Their Promise

The second reason why so many of the Jewish people were remaining outside the gates of the kingdom, Paul went on to explain, was because the Jews had stumbled over the gospel promise by trying to establish their own righteousness by the works of the law:

> What shall we say, then? That Gentiles who did not pursue righteousness have attained it, that is, a righteousness that is by faith; but that Israel who pursued a law that would lead to righteousness did not succeed in reaching that law. Why? Because they did not pursue it by faith, but as if it were based on works. They have stumbled over the stumbling stone, as it is written, "Behold, I am laying in Zion a stone of stumbling, and a rock of offense; and whoever believes in him will not be put to shame" (Rom. 9:30-33).

The Jews were given both the gospel and the law. The gospel promised that the seed of Abraham would establish righteousness and bring blessings to the world, and the law explained what was required from the promised seed for this promise to be fulfilled. Rather than trusting in the gospel and looking by faith at the righteousness that would be established by the promised seed (i.e., the Messiah), the Jews sought to establish their own righteousness by thinking they were the promised seed:

> Brothers, my heart's desire and prayer to God for them is that they may be saved. For I bear them witness that they have a zeal for God, but not according to knowledge. For, being ignorant of the righteousness of God, and seeking to establish their own, they did not submit to God's righteousness (Rom. 10:1-3).

The Jews were blinded by pride. They were using the law, which was given to kill their self-righteousness and point them to faith in Christ, as an instrument to establish their own righteousness. They were blinded to the righteousness that comes by faith because they were zealous in trying to establish their own righteousness by the law.

The Gentiles, on the other hand, who were not seeking righteousness, gained the righteousness of Christ by faith. The Jews were tripping over the promise by trying to keep the law, while the Gentiles were looking to the promise by faith because they had no pretense of thinking they could keep the law: "For Christ is the end of the law for righteousness to everyone who believes" (Rom. 10:4). Christ did not come to call law-keepers but sinners to repentance (Mk. 2:17). For this reason, the Jews were being left out while the Gentiles were rushing into the kingdom.

After explaining the nature of the law and promise, Paul concluded by stating,

> For the Scripture says, "Everyone who believes in him will not be put to shame." For there is no distinction between Jew and Greek; for the same Lord is Lord of all, bestowing his riches on all who call on him. For "everyone who calls on the name of the Lord will be saved" (Rom. 10:11-13).

The Jews were surrounded by the gospel. "But I ask, have they not heard? Indeed they have, for 'Their voice has gone out to all the earth, and their words to the ends of the world'" (Rom. 10:18). Yet, it was the Gentiles who were apprehending the gospel by faith: "I have been found by those who did not seek me; I have shown myself to those who did not ask for me" (Rom. 10:20). Israel, on the other hand, had the gospel from their inception, and yet generation after generation they continued to stubbornly reject it in unbelief: "But of Israel he says, 'All day long I have held out my hands to a disobedient and contrary people'" (Rom. 10:21).

Made Jealous by Foreigners

There was also a third reason why the Gentiles were coming into the kingdom at a faster rate than were the Jews. God had purposed to make the Jewish people jealous by the Gentiles: "But I ask, did Israel not understand? First Moses says, 'I will make you jealous of those who are not a nation; with a foolish nation I will make you angry'" (Rom. 10:19). For this to happen, Gentiles needed to outnumber the Jews.

Has God Completely Abandoned the Jews?

We could imagine the Jewish reader, at this point, would be feeling discouraged. Paul was seeking to humble the Jews by prompting them to not trust in their circumcision, their law, or their ancestry. Paul also explained that the kingdom of God is not characterized by ethnic Israel, for Gentiles could enter the gates of the promised kingdom without even identifying themselves with the Jewish people.

Moreover, Paul went on explain the various reasons why Gentiles were pressing into the kingdom, and the Jews were remaining outside its gates. With all the nations of the world flooding into the kingdom, the kingdom would not even look Jewish before long. At that point in the letter, the Jews may have concluded that God had utterly forsaken them. In response to this notion, Paul gave four proofs, found in Romans 11, that physical Israel had not been totally abandoned by God.

Paul Is Proof that God Has Not Completely Abandoned the Jews

First, Paul himself was proof there was still hope for the Jewish people: "I ask, then, has God rejected his people? By no means! For I myself am an Israelite, a descendant of Abraham, a member of the tribe of Benjamin" (Rom. 11:1).

Election Is Proof that God Has Not Completely Abandoned the Jews

Second, God has not totally abandoned the Jewish people, for there is still a remnant among them who are chosen by God unto salvation:

> God has not rejected his people whom he foreknew. Do you not know what the Scripture says of Elijah, how he appeals to God against Israel? "Lord, they have killed your prophets, they have demolished your altars, and I alone am left, and they seek my life." But what is God's reply to him? "I have kept for myself seven thousand men who have not bowed the knee to Baal." So too at the present time there is a remnant, chosen by grace (Rom. 11:2-5).

Even though the great majority of Jews are rejecting their Messiah, that does not mean that God has totally abandoned them. Even in the Old Testament era, grace was never bestowed upon every Israelite. Salvation has always been by grace, and grace has always been reserved for only a chosen remnant out of Israel. The greater part of the Jewish people was just as faithless then as they are now. As there was only a chosen remnant by grace then, so there remains a chosen remnant by grace now.

The Gospel Reaching the Gentiles Is Proof that God Has Not Completely Abandoned the Jews

Third, we know God has not totally abandoned the Jews because He has chosen to use the Gentile reception of the gospel as a means to prompt the Jews to faith in Christ: "So I ask, did they stumble in order that they might fall? By no means! Rather through their trespass salvation has come to the Gentiles, so as to make Israel jealous" (Rom. 11:11). Though the promises belonged to the Jews, the Gentiles were the ones enjoying the inheritance. Seeing the Gentiles receive what was promised to the Jews was designed to lead the Jews to faith in Christ. Therefore Paul, with his great love for the Jews, was happy to be a missionary to the Gentiles. Paul knew that by reaching the Gentiles he would indirectly be reaching the Jews: "Now I am speaking to you Gentiles. Inasmuch then as I am an apostle to the Gentiles, I magnify my ministry in order somehow to make my fellow Jews jealous, and thus save some of them" (Rom. 11:13-14).

It is important to note the circular rotation of the gospel, starting with the Jews, then going to the Gentiles, and then returning again to the Jews. First, the gospel originally belonged to the Jews. Second, the unbelief of the Jews led Jewish missionaries to turn to the Gentiles. Third, the gospel coming to the Gentiles is meant to prompt jealousy in the Jews, thus making them more receptive to the gospel, even when brought by Gentile missionaries! Just as God used the Jews' rejection of the gospel to bring the gospel to the Gentiles, God is using the reception of the gospel by the Gentiles to bring the gospel back to the Jews.

Following this, Paul turns from comforting the Jews to warning the Gentiles not to start boasting. If the Jews have no right to boast as the people group to whom the gospel was originally given, then the Gentiles have even less room to boast as the beneficiaries of the Jewish rejection of the gospel:

> But if some of the branches were broken off, and you, although a wild olive shoot, were grafted in among the others and now share in the nourishing root of the olive tree, do not be arrogant toward the branches. If you are, remember it is not you who support the root, but the root that supports you. Then you will say, "Branches were broken off so that I might be grafted in." That is true. They were broken off because of their unbelief, but you stand fast through faith. So do not become proud, but fear. For if God did not spare the natural branches, neither will he spare you (Rom. 11:17-22).

As this is true, the question must be asked: has God turned completely away from the Jewish people? No. Paul's conversion is proof that God is still saving Jews. There is still a remnant out of Israel which has been chosen by grace unto salvation. According to Paul, it was a part of God's eternal plan to stimulate Jewish converts by bringing the gospel to the Gentiles. Chapters 9-11 of Romans not only explain that God has not totally abandoned physical Israel; they also explain the method God has chosen to save His elect from out of physical Israel. Yet if salvation is not by birthright, circumcision, or Jewish ethnicity, then how does an ethnic Jew become a member of spiritual Israel? What is the divine process? Chapter 9 explains that it is not Jewish ethnicity, but divine election, that determines who receives the promised inheritance. Chapter 10 says it is not through observance of the law, but by faith in the gospel, that the inheritance of Abraham is received. Chapter 11 shows how the gospel will have a positive effect upon the Jews as it is being received by the Gentiles.

Thus, Paul proved that God has not totally abandoned physical Israel by explaining the process in which the elect remnant of physical Israel will be saved. In short, the Jewish remnant that God has chosen to save will be brought into the promised kingdom (1) by election, (2) by the gospel, and (3) by being provoked by the Gentiles to jealousy. "And in this way all Israel will be saved" (Rom. 11:26a).[8]

The Irrevocable Nature of the Gospel Is Proof that God Has Not Completely Abandoned the Jews

Fourth, after explaining the method God uses to call the Jewish remnant unto salvation, Paul provided one more theological proof that God had not totally abandoned the Jews:

> [A]s it is written, "The Deliverer will come from Zion, he will banish ungodliness from Jacob"; "and this will be my covenant with them when I take away their sins." As regards the gospel, they are enemies of God for your sake. But as regards election, they are beloved for the sake of their forefathers (Rom. 11:26b-28).

God had given the Jews a promise, and that promise remains true for all those who receive it by faith: "For the gifts and the calling of God are irrevocable" (Rom. 11:29). The

---

[8] The phrase "And in this way all Israel will be saved" is to be understood as "in this manner, or on this wise" (*The Complete Word Study Dictionary: New Testament.* Gen. Ed. Spiros Zodhiates, Chattanooga, TN: AMG, 1992, 1078). Paul was not predicting a particular timeframe in which the gospel would go back to Israel nor that there would be a point in time when all physical Jews will be saved. This would have undermined everything he said previously. Rather, all elect Israelites will be saved in the way he described. This is confirmed by the verses that follow (Rom. 11:30- 32).

promise stands, and it may still be received by any Jew who places his or her trust in Christ. In this regard, there is no difference between Jews and Gentiles.

Jews and Gentiles Are Tied Together by Christ

The sum of Paul's view of the two seeds of Abraham can be seen in Romans 15. This chapter builds on what was said previously throughout the book, connecting the major tenets of Paul's covenantal position.

First, there is a distinction between Abraham's physical and spiritual seed, a distinction that should not be confused.

Second, only Abraham's spiritual seed inherit the promised blessings.

Third, Abraham's spiritual seed include both physical Jews and Gentiles who have faith in Christ.

Fourth, the promise given to Abraham was based upon a condition that was fulfilled in Christ: "For I tell you that Christ became a servant to the circumcised to show God's truthfulness, in order to confirm the promises given to the patriarchs" (Rom. 15:8).

Fifth, the promises, in Christ, have been opened up to the nations of the world. As God promised Abraham that in his seed all the nations of the world would be blessed, Christ, by fulfilling the legal condition of the Abrahamic Covenant, has opened up the promised kingdom to the Gentiles:

> For I tell you that Christ became a servant to the circumcised to show God's truthfulness, in order to confirm the promises given to the patriarchs, and in order that the Gentiles might glorify God for his mercy. As it is written, "Therefore I will praise you among the Gentiles, and sing to your name." And again it is said, "Rejoice, O Gentiles, with

his people." And again, "Praise the Lord, all you Gentiles, and let all the peoples extol him." And again Isaiah says, "The root of Jesse will come, even he who arises to rule the Gentiles; in him will the Gentiles hope" (Rom. 15:8-12).

Sixth, the church does not replace Israel. Rather, believing Gentiles are grafted into the same tree with believing Jews. That is, Gentiles do not enjoy a different inheritance but share in the same inheritance that was promised to Abraham and his seed. As Paul specifically indicates later in the chapter, "the Gentiles have come to share in their spiritual blessings" (Rom. 15:27).

Seventh, just because the gospel has gone from the Jews to the Gentiles does not mean God has completely abandoned the Jews. The gospel still belongs to the Jews, and just like the Gentiles, Jews may inherit the promises at any time through faith in Christ Jesus.

Conclusion

God gave the gospel to Abraham by promising Abraham that in his seed all the nations of the world would be blessed. This blessing would be free to those who believe, but it placed Abraham's physical seed under the legal obligation to obey God. Although all of Abraham's descendants were born under this impossibly heavy obligation, there was a way out of the condemnation of the law. This was found in the one physical seed, Christ Jesus, who fulfilled the requirements of the law. Therefore, for the rest of the physical seed of Abraham, the only way to be delivered from the wrath of God was for them to place their faith in the promised seed, Christ Jesus, rather than trying to fulfill the condition for themselves. The dichotomous nature of the Abrahamic Covenant is borne out by the wording of the covenant, the actual fulfillment of the covenant, and the Pauline interpretation of the covenant.

8

The Separation of Law and Gospel

The essence of the Covenant of Works is the moral law. The Covenant of Works was established with all humanity in Adam. The moral law is written on the conscience of every person. It is non-negotiable, and it cannot be altered or amended. The Covenant of Works explains what God requires of us. Divine justice demands that everyone, including Jesus Christ, stands either justified or condemned by God's law. Everywhere we see the law, along with its promises and curses, we see the Covenant of Works.[1]

---

[1] The moral law of God as revealed in the conscience, in the garden of Eden, or anywhere else in redemptive history is all the light that is needed for one to uncover the ingredients of the Covenant of Works. This is because the law and the Covenant of Works are essentially the same. Both the Covenant of Works and the law have blessings and curses, are unilaterally given to man by God, and are legal and forensic in nature. They are both relational in nature because the same law that demands loving relationships with God and our neighbors also warns of legal justice for all covenant/relationship breakers. Therefore, in this sense, wherever we see God's moral law imposed upon man, we see all the major elements of the Covenant of Works. As John Frame states: "When you have a lord and a servant, you have a covenant" (*Systematic Theology*, Phillipsburg, NJ: P&R, 2013, 62).

Yet what about the Covenant of Grace? The Covenant of Grace only exists because the man Christ Jesus has stepped in and fulfilled the Covenant of Works for those whom He represents. Without the fulfillment of the Covenant of Works, there can be no Covenant of Grace. It is a Covenant of Grace only for those who are justified by faith without the deeds of the law. It was a Covenant of Works for Christ because He had to live and die a righteous man. Believers are justified by the law, but only because Christ obeyed the law for them. Therefore, whenever we talk about the Covenant of Grace in redemptive history, we must never neglect to observe the ongoing administration of the Covenant of Works.

What is the relationship between the Covenant of Works and the Covenant of Grace? The Covenant of Grace is the Covenant of Works fulfilled in Jesus Christ for all those who believe. As Charles Alexander stated:

> What is to us a covenant of grace, was to our glorious Mediator, a Covenant of Works and death and condemnation. On the one hand He fulfilled the obligations of obedience which man had never rendered, and on the other He expiated on the tree, by awful death, the offence which had brought down the curse... What was death to Christ became life to us. What was Law and Justice to Him, became grace and life and immortality to us.[2]

Meditation on such a glorious truth led Oliver Cromwell to exclaim on his deathbed, "The two covenants are one."[3] So while there is a single covenant, there are two dimensions (works and grace) to that covenant. Some are united to the last Adam, who is the one and only covenant keeper, while others remain united to the first Adam. We are under grace or law

---

[2] Charles D. Alexander, *Revelation Spiritually Understood*, April 20, 2013, available at: http://www.allbygrace.com/alexrev047-14.html

[3] Alexander, *Revelation Spiritually Understood*.

depending upon where we stand with Christ Jesus. Faith or lack of faith in Christ determines if the Covenant of Works condemns or justifies us.

Understanding the organic relationship between the Covenant of Works and the Covenant of Grace is important but understanding the distinctions between them is fundamentally necessary. It is eternally destructive if we confuse works with grace.[4]

Confusing Grace with Works

The Abrahamic Covenant promised grace to the nations by promising that the law would be fulfilled in the Seed of Abraham. Salvation was dependent upon the Jews (Jn. 4:22). As we read the narrative of the Old Testament, we notice that the Jews, though they were promised the gospel, were born under the law. The only way out of their conditional standing before God was for them to reject their own righteousness and trust in the unconditional promise that was given to them in the Abrahamic Covenant.

Covenantal Presbyterians, however, deny that the physical children of Abraham were born under the Covenant of Works. Rather they claim that the physical children of Abraham were born into the Covenant of Grace.

---

[4] John Colquhoun (1748-1827) warned of the danger of confusing law and grace together: "There can be no evangelical holiness, either of heart or of life, unless it proceeds from faith working by love; and no true faith either of the law or of the gospel unless the leading distinctions between the one and the other are spiritually discerned... To blend or confound them has been a fatal source of error in the Christian Church and has embarrassed many believers not a little in their exercise of faith and practice of holiness. Troubled consciences cannot ordinarily be quieted unless the doctrine of the gospel is rightly distinguished form that of the law" (*A Treatise on the Law and the Gospel*, Grand Rapids: 2009, XXIX).

However, if Abraham's physical seed were born into the Covenant of Grace, then how could it have been possible for them to break the covenant? How could the Covenant of Grace be breakable? Because covenantal Presbyterians recognize covenant breakers in the Old Covenant, they must find a way to introduce conditions and covenant breakers into the Covenant of Grace. In so doing, covenantal Presbyterians are forced to mixed law with grace.

Forcing conditions and covenant breakers into the Covenant of Grace, however, is the fatal flaw Presbyterian Covenantalism.[5] And Presbyterians do not have a consistent and unified answer for this dilemma. Many Presbyterians have admitted that it is hard to reconcile covenant breakers with the Covenant of Grace. For instance, Anthony Burgess confessed, "I do not find in any point of Divinity, learned men so confused and perplexed (being like Abraham's Ram, hung in a bush of briars and brambles by the head) as here."[6] Affirming this predicament, Peter Golding stated,

> This is one of the most difficult problems in theology... One of the main reasons why Reformed theologians did not favour speaking of the covenant as being confined to the elect only in every sense of the term is because "this would make no allowance for the fact of covenant- breakers."[7]

Henri Blocher, a credobaptist, was right when he claimed this is "the thorn in the flesh of many covenant theologians."[8]

---

[5] See Jeffrey D. Johnson, *The Fatal Flaw of the Theology Behind Infant Baptism* (Conway, AR: Free Grace Press, 2010).

[6] Anthony Burgess, cited in Brenton C. Ferry, "Works in the Mosaic Covenant: A Reformed Taxonomy," in *The Law is Not Faith: Essays on Works and Grace in the Mosaic Covenant*, editors, Bryan D. Estelle, J. V. Fesko, and David VanDrunen (Phillipsburg, NJ: P&R, 2009), 76.

[7] Peter Golding, *Covenant Theology* (Glasgow, UK: Mentor, 2004), 128-129.

[8] Henri Blocher, 'Old *Covenant, New Covenant*', in A. T. B. McGowan, ed., *Always Reforming* (Downers Grove, IL: IVP, 2006), 249.

Blocher went on to state: "'Reformed theologians found abundant evidence that fundamentally the Covenant of Grace is a covenant established with those who are in Christ.' Yet, at the same time, they wished to include the children of believers, among whom there are a number of non-elect, after the promise 'You and your seed.'"[9]

The answer to this problem would be simple if Presbyterians did not succumb to the pressure of hanging onto infant baptism. Until they are ready to abandon infant baptism, they must continue to mix Abraham's physical seed, conditions, and covenant breakers with the Covenant of Grace.

Regrettably, John Murray's solution was to bring grace and works together in his *covenantal nomism*.[10] Murray understood that the Abrahamic Covenant involved both grace and works.[11] However, rather than properly separating the grace that belongs to Abraham's spiritual seed from the conditions that belong to Abrahams physical seed, he placed the same group of people under grace and law at the same time.

Murray did this by stating that Abraham's physical seed were born into the covenant by grace, but they would only remain in the covenant by works. For Murray, entrance into the covenant was by grace alone: "The necessity of keeping the covenant on the part of men does not interfere with the divine monergism of dispensation. The necessity of keeping is but the expression of the magnitude of the grace bestowed and the

---

[9] Blocher, "Old Covenant, New Covenant," 249.
[10] As E. P. Sanders explains, "Covenantal nomism is the view that one's place in God's plan is established on the basis of the covenant and that the covenant requires as the proper response of man his obedience to its commandments" (Sanders, *Paul and Palestinian Judaism: A Comparison of Patterns of Religion*. Philadelphia: Fortress, 1977, 75).
[11] See John Murray, *The Covenant of Grace* (Phillipsburg, NJ: P&R, 1988), 18.

spirituality of the relation constituted."[12] Yet Murray went on to state: "The continued enjoyment of this grace and the relation established is contingent upon the fulfillment of certain conditions."[13]

According to Murray, the Covenant of Grace is entered into by grace but maintained by works. Murray was unambiguous about this when he said, "For apart from the fulfillment of these conditions the grace bestowed and the relation established are meaningless," Murray concluded, "By breaking the covenant what is broken is not the condition of bestowal but the condition of consummated fruition."[14]

Covenantal nomism was also advanced by John Murray's successor at Westminster Theological Seminary (Philadelphia), Norman Shepherd. Shepherd's theology, in turn, was a catalyst for what is now known as the Federal Vision, a theological system that combines the Covenant of Works with the Covenant of Grace by rejecting the historic Reformation distinction between law and gospel. Federal Vision is promoted today by men such as Steve Schlissel and Rich Lusk. Schlissel states, "This law/Gospel dichotomy is a false one. It is unbiblical."[15]

Covenantal nomism is fatally dangerous because it adds something to the finished work of Christ. It is true that we see both gospel and law throughout the Old Testament, but once we mix the two together and add conditions to the covenant of

---

[12] Murray, *The Covenant of Grace*, 18.

[13] Murray, *The Covenant of Grace*, 18.

[14] Murray, *The Covenant of Grace*, 18. Mark W. Karlberg states: "Murray's interpretation of the Mosaic Covenant marks a dead-end, the end of the line in English-Puritan interpretation. His position is exegetically and theologically untenable" *(Federalism and the Westminster Tradition*, 23-24).

[15] Citied in Guy Waters, *The Federal Vision and Covenant Theology: A Comparative Analysis* (Phillipsburg, NJ: P&R, 2006), 51.

grace, we have distorted the gospel in the same way the Judaizers did by adding circumcision to the gospel equation.

Confusing Abraham's Physical Seed with Abraham's Spiritual Seed

Covenantal nomism is the natural outworking of the core presupposition behind Presbyterian covenant theology. If the physical seed of believers belong to the Covenant of Grace, then conditions must also belong to the Covenant of Grace. Thankfully, most Presbyterian covenantal systems are inconsistent and do not blend works with grace in their doctrine of justification.

Nevertheless, all covenantal Presbyterians mix the membership of the Covenant of Works with the membership of the Covenant of Grace. If paedobaptists desire to remain faithful to their presupposition that Abraham's physical seed are born into the membership of the Covenant of Grace, they must also state that covenant breakers belong to the Covenant of Grace.

However, this presupposition mixes Abraham's physical seed with Abraham's spiritual seed, combining those who belong to the Covenant of Works with those who belong to the covenant of grace. More importantly, this mixes those who are united to the first Adam with those who are united to the second Adam. This means covenant breakers are somehow members of the Covenant of Grace and the Covenant of Works at the same time.[16]

The following statement by John Owen, made earlier in his ministry, is an example of this special mixing of the covenants, for in this statement he failed to distinguish between

---

[16] This implies that Christ does not legally represent all who are in the Covenant of Grace. Or, even worse, this implies that Christ is a poor representative for some under His legal care.

Abraham's physical and spiritual seed.[17] Owen claimed, "[T]he promises made unto the fathers were, that their infant seed, their buds and offspring, should have an equal share in the covenant with them." From this Owen concluded, "[T]he children of believing parents, who have avouched God's covenant, as the church of Israel did, Exod. 24:7, 8, have the same right and interest with their parents in the covenant."[18]

Owen started out with the term seed referring to the natural descendants of Abraham and ended with the term referring to the natural descendants of the spiritual descendants of Abraham. He and other Paedobaptists make this switch without any biblical warrant.

If the term seed is referring to Abraham's natural seed, it is limited to the Jews only. Why? Because the physical seed of Gentile believers cannot be counted among Abraham's natural offspring. Thus, being a child of Christian parents does not make an infant a part of ethnic Israel.

On the other hand, if the term seed is referring to Abraham's spiritual seed, then this rules out all those who are

---

[17] By the time Owen wrote the first volume to his commentary on Hebrews (1668), he would argue against mixing the physical and spiritual seed of Abraham together: "It is true, the former carnal privilege of Abraham and his posterity expiring, on the grounds before mentioned, the ordinances of worship which were suited thereunto did necessarily cease also. And this cast the Jews into great perplexities, and proved the last trial that God made of them; for whereas both these,—namely, the carnal and spiritual privileges of Abraham's covenant,—had been carried on together in a mixed way for many generations, coming now to be separated, and a trial to be made (Malachi 3) who of the Jews had interest in both, who in one only, those who had only the carnal privilege, of being children of Abraham according to the flesh, contended for a share on that single account in the other also,–that is, in all the promises annexed unto the covenant. But the foundation of their plea was taken away, and the church, unto which the promises belong, remained with them that were heirs of Abraham's faith only" (*An Exposition of the Epistle to the Hebrews*, 1:151).

[18] John Owen, "Of Infant Baptism and Dipping," in *The Works of John Owen*, Vol. 16. (Edinburgh: Banner of Truth Trust, 1998), 262.

not born of the Spirit. Thus, unbelieving Jews have no more claim to Abraham as their spiritual father than the stones of the earth (Matt. 3:9). Nehemiah Coxe understood this when he stated:

> For this whole covenant of circumcision given to the carnal seed, can no more convey spiritual and eternal blessings to them as such, than it can now enright a believer (though a child of Abraham) in their temporal and typical blessings in the land of Canaan.[19]

The distinction between Abraham's natural and spiritual seed sounds simple enough, but it is confounded by Presbyterians. As David Kingdon remarks, "The New Testament nowhere allows us to operate with the concept of a literal seed in the context of the church, but this is just what Paedobaptists constantly try to do."[20]

By artificially placing the physical seed of Abraham, conditions, and covenant breakers into the Covenant of Grace, covenantal Presbyterians look at the Abrahamic Covenant as a one-dimensional covenant of grace. They then try to work around this inconsistency by devising a form of two-dimensional (external and internal) covenant membership. Nevertheless, the external membership remains conditional and breakable, which looks nothing like the biblical covenant of grace.

Yet this inconsistency does not exist when we properly understand the dichotomous nature of the Abrahamic Covenant, for it promised the gospel by placing the physical seed of Abraham under a legal condition that was satisfied by Christ Jesus. Only when Abraham's physical seed looked to

---

[19] Coxe, *Covenant Theology*, 93
[20] David Kingdon, *Children of Abraham* (Sussex, UK: Carey Publications, 1973), 53.

the promise by faith were they justified, and that independently from their ethnicity, circumcision, and observance of the law. In other words, the unbelieving physical seed of Abraham were never naturally born into the Covenant of Grace. G. H. Kersten was right when he stated, "So it is far from correct to say that the covenant [of grace] was made with Abraham's natural seed."[21]

If covenantal Paedobaptists would refrain from mixing Abraham's physical seed with Abraham's spiritual seed, their inconsistency would be resolved. This is why Nehemiah Coxe stated that "there is no way of avoiding confusion and entanglements in our conception of these things except by keeping before our eyes the distinction between Abraham's seed as either spiritual or carnal, and of the respective promises belonging to each."[22]

Charles Hodge, though a committed Presbyterian, understood many of the theological problems of confusing both the Covenant of Works with the Covenant of Grace and the physical seed with the spiritual seed of Abraham:

> It is to be remembered that there were two covenants made with Abraham. By the one, his natural descendants through Isaac were constituted a commonwealth, an external, visible community. By the other, his spiritual descendants were constituted a church. The parties to the former covenant were God and the nation; to the other, God, and His true people. The promises of the national covenant were

---

[21] G. H. Kersten, *Reformed Dogmatics*, 2 vols., (Grand Rapids: HeuleGordon, 2009), 1:236. Words in brackets are mine. Kersten is one of the few covenantal Paedobaptists to deny that the natural children of Abraham were born into the Covenant of Grace. Kersten understood the theological implications of including the non-elect children of Abraham in the Covenant of Grace. According to Kersten, "if the Covenant of Grace were also made with the non-elect, Christ would also have become a Surety for them, and would have shed His blood for reprobates" (1:236).

[22] Coxe, *Covenant Theology*, 93.

national blessings; the promises of the spiritual covenant (i.e., the Covenant of Grace) were spiritual blessings, reconciliation, holiness, and eternal life. The conditions of the one covenant were circumcision and obedience to the law; the conditions of the other were, and ever have been, faith in the Messiah, as the seed of the woman, the Son of God, the Saviour of the world. There cannot be a greater mistake than to confound the national covenant with the Covenant of Grace, [that is, the Old Covenant with the new] and the commonwealth founded on the one, with the church founded on the other. When Christ came, the commonwealth was abolished, and there was nothing put in its place. The church remained. There was no external covenant, nor promise of external blessings, on condition of external rites, and subjection. There was a spiritual society, with spiritual promises, on condition of faith in Christ. The church is, therefore, in its essential nature, a company of believers, and not an external society, requiring merely external profession as the condition of membership.[23]

I cannot fully reconcile Hodge's statement above with his belief in infant baptism, for a committed covenantal Baptist could not have given a more precise explanation of the dichotomous nature of the Abrahamic Covenant.[24] This distinction is at the very heart of Baptist covenant theology.

The Unity of the Abrahamic Covenant

Although much has been said about the dichotomous nature of the Abrahamic Covenant, the Abrahamic Covenant is not

---

[23] Charles Hodge, *Discussions in Church Polity* (New York: Scribner, 1878), 66-67.

[24] I suppose Hodge left the door open for infant baptism by claiming the Old Covenant was concerned only with natural and temporal blessings, while the New Covenant is concerned about spiritual blessings. Yet this is not the case. At the heart of the Old Covenant was life and death, which was signified by circumcision.

two separate covenants but a single covenant. Yes, the Abrahamic Covenant had unconditional and conditional aspects, and it promised both physical and spiritual blessings, and it contained both physical and spiritual seed. However, both dimensions are ultimately fulfilled in a single person—Christ Jesus, who perfectly unites the physical and spiritual aspects of the covenant.

God promised Abraham a righteous kingdom. Abraham's children were to be as numerous as the stars and heirs to the world (Rom. 4:13). Yet because Abraham's natural offspring were unable to obey the condition of the covenant, they were merely a foreshadowing of the coming fulfillment. The natural children of Abraham were never fully able to subdue Canaan, falling short of establishing a righteous kingdom and finding eschatological rest. Just as Ishmael was not the fulfillment of the promised seed, so the Israelites as a nation proved not to be the fulfillment either (Gal. 4:25, 30).

Yet, as we have seen, Israel's failure does not mean the Abrahamic Covenant consisted of an empty promise. In the fullness of time, God sent Abraham a Seed that satisfied both the physical and spiritual, the conditional and unconditional, aspects of the Abrahamic Covenant. All the promises are fulfilled in Christ Jesus.

Those who are united to Christ by faith (both Jews and Gentiles) not only become the spiritual seed of Abraham, but they also eagerly wait, as Abraham did, to inherit the Promised Land. The meek shall inherit the earth, but only after Christ has subdued all His enemies under His footstool and has brought all people and nations to bow to His Lordship (Phil. 2:9-11).

Then, after Christ returns, heaven and earth will be united in the coming of the new heavens and the new earth where only righteousness dwells. At that time, God's people will receive their new, glorified bodies and find eschatological rest as the fullness of both the natural and spiritual aspects of the Abrahamic Covenant are fulfilled in the consummation of the kingdom of God in the eternal age to come. The kingdom promised to Abraham was both spiritual and physical in nature, but it only consists of those who have been united to Christ by faith.

Conclusion

This brings us back to our original objective: answering the question, who are the people of God—Israel or the church? As the progenitor of the holy, Messianic Seed, Israel was the people group to whom the gospel was entrusted. Yet they were placed under a legal condition that they could never fulfill. By faith, however, the Jews can exit the Covenant of Works and become members of the Covenant of Grace. This also means, however, that apart from faith, the Jews remain the children of darkness and will be condemned for their sins on the Day of Judgment.

On the other hand, the believing church is the true people of God and the fulfillment of the Abrahamic Covenant because the true Israel of God has always consisted of believers and believers alone.

Appendix

The Fatal Flaw of the New Perspective(s) of Paul

Understanding the dichotomous nature of the Abrahamic Covenant is helpful because many accomplished theologians (e.g., E. P. Sanders, James Dunn, and N. T. Wright) have been tripped up in their understanding of justification due to their failure to understand how the unconditional promise of the covenant affected its conditional requirement.

For instance, after exhaustive research of the primary sources of Second Temple Judaism, E. P. Sanders constructed a system known as "covenantal nomism" where God's people enter the covenant by grace, but they remain in the covenant by works. Adherents of first-century Judaism, according to Sanders, viewed their election as God's covenantal people as an act of grace, but they also viewed their continued enjoyment of the blessings of the covenant as being dependent upon their national obedience to the law of God.[1]

---

[1] See E. P. Sanders, *Paul and Palestinian Judaism* (Philadelphia, PA: Fortress Press, 1977).

This was no doubt a part of the misconstrued theology of first century Judaism. With the dichotomous nature of the Abrahamic Covenant in mind, it would be easy to imagine how unbelieving Jews would fail to separate the unconditional and conditional elements of the covenant and thus construct a false theological system that conflates grace and works.

Nevertheless, the problem with Sanders is that he sought to impose the grace/works synthesis of covenantal nomism upon the writings of Moses, as if Moses also taught covenantal nomism. The basic error of Sanders and his followers is the assumption that Second Temple Judaism held a correct interpretation of the writings of Moses.[2]

Nevertheless, following the research of Sanders, James Dunn sought to reinterpret the writings of the apostle Paul considering the covenantal nomism of Second Temple Judaism. According to Dunn, Paul's argument against the Judaizers was not centered on personal salvation and works righteousness.[3]

Rather, the Jews of that period were merely concerned about upholding the Jewish boundary markers (circumcision, dietary laws, etc.) that fenced off who did and did not belong to God's covenantal people. Therefore, according to Dunn, the "works of the law," to which Paul was opposed, were not referring to general moral obedience to God's law, but to the specific Jewish boundary markers that the Jews were seeking

---

[2] Sadly, John Murray also read covenantal nomism back into the writings of Moses. See John Murray, The Covenant of Grace (Phillipsburg, NJ: P&R, 1988), 18-22. This led men like Norman Shepherd to construct a misrepresentation of biblical justification similar to that of the New Perspective on Paul. Now Shepherd's view has been developed into what is now known as the "Federal Vision." For my treatment of Federal Vision, see my book, *The Fatal Flaw of the Theology Behind Infant Baptism* (Conway, AR: Free Grace Press, 2010), 109-119.

[3] See James Dunn, The Theology of Paul the Apostle (Grand Rapids: Eerdmans, 1998).

to enforce upon the believing Gentiles. Thus, in Dunn's view, Paul was not against covenantal nomism (i.e., a covenant and a justification that requires works), but rather Paul was against the idea that Gentiles had to become Jewish proselytes and follow Jewish customs before they can be identified as members of God's covenantal people.

I substantially agree with Sanders and Dunn that the form of Judaism that Paul was seeking to confront was not that of an altogether legalistic works righteousness theology, but rather that of an ethnocentric law/grace synthesis. This fusion can be discerned when Paul connects circumcision, along with other Jewish boundary markers, with a view of works righteousness (Phil. 3:4-6).

Yet, I disagree with Sanders and Dunn that Moses or Paul sanctioned covenantal nomism. This is because, in both the writings of Moses and the writings of the apostle Paul, God's covenants are based either upon works or upon grace, never a mixture of the two.

According to the theology of Paul, adding the works of the law to the equation of justification, whether in the context of Jewish ethnocentrism or not, nullifies the doctrines of grace alone, Christ alone, and faith alone.

Blending law and grace is theologically dangerous. Yet if we keep the promise and the condition (along with the spiritual and physical seeds of the Abrahamic Covenant) distinct from each other, then the difficultly is safely resolved. We do not have to blend the Covenant of Grace with the Covenant of Works, as covenantal nomism does. We must remember that the spiritual seed was promised the blessings of the covenant of grace by means of the fulfillment of the Covenant of Works by the physical seed—Jesus Christ.

When this is recognized, it can be seen that the unbelieving physical seed of Abraham were never members of the Covenant of Grace, even though they received many fringe benefits from having been part of nation chosen by God to be the progenitor of the Messiah.

Bibliography

Alexander, Charles D. *Revelation Spiritually Understood, Part 14: The Mystery of God Complete.* April 20, 2013, available at: http://www.allbygrace.com/alexrev047-14.html.

Alexander, Desmond T. *From Eden to the New Jerusalem: An Introduction to Biblical Theology.* Grand Rapids: Kregel, 2008.

Beale, G. K. *A New Testament Biblical Theology: The Unfolding of the Old Testament in the New.* Grand Rapids: Baker, 2011.

———. *The Temple and the Church's Mission: A Biblical Theology of the Dwelling Place of God.* Downers Grove, IL: IVP, 2004.

Beeke, Joel and Mark Jones. *A Puritan Theology.* Grand Rapids: Reformation Heritage Books, 2012.

Berkhof, Louis. *Systematic Theology.* Grand Rapids: Eerdmans, 1994.

Blocher, Henri. "Old Covenant, New Covenant." *Always Reforming.* McGowan, A. T. B., ed. Downers Grove, IL: IVP, 2006.

Brown, Michael. *Christ and the Condition: The Covenant Theology of Samuel Petto (1624-1711)*. Grand Rapids: Reformation Heritage Books, 2012.

Calvin, John. *Institutes of the Christian Religion*. Trans. by Ford Lewis Battles. McNeill, John T., ed. The Library of Christian Classics. Philadelphia, PA: Westminster Press, 1977.

Chantry, Walter. "The Covenants of Works and Grace." *Covenant Theology: A Baptist Distinctive*. Birmingham, AL: Solid Ground Christian Books, 2013.

Colquhoun, John. *A Treatise on the Law and the Gospel*. Grand Rapids: Soli Deo Gloria, 2009.

Coxe, Nehemiah. "A Discourse of the Covenants that God Made with Men before the Law." *Covenant Theology: From Adam to Christ*. Miller, Ronald D., Francisco Orozco, and James M. Renihan, eds. Palmdale, CA: Reformed Baptist Academic Press, 2005.

Denault, Pascal. *The Distinctiveness of Baptist Covenant Theology: A Comparison between Seventeenth-Century Particular Baptist and Paedobaptist Federalism*. Birmingham, AL: Solid Ground Christian Books, 2013.

Duguid, Iain M. "Covenant Nomism and the Exile." *Covenant, Justification, and Pastoral Ministry*. Clark, R. Scott, ed. Phillipsburg, NJ: P & R Publishing, 2007.

Dunn, James. *The Theology of Paul the Apostle*. Grand Rapids: Eerdmans, 1998.

Edwards, Jonathan. *A History of the Work of Redemption*. Edinburgh, UK: Banner of Truth, 2003.

Estelle, Bryan D., J. V. Fesko and David VanDrunen, eds. *The Law is Not of Faith: Essays on Works and Grace in the Mosaic Covenant.* Phillipsburg, NJ: P & R Publishing, 2009.

Ferry, Brenton C. "Works in the Mosaic Covenant: A Reformed Taxonomy." *The Law is Not of Faith: Essays on Works and Grace in the Mosaic Covenant.* Estelle, Bryan D., J. V. Fesko, and David VanDrunen, eds. Phillipsburg, NJ: P & R Publishing, 2009.

Fisher, Edward. *The Marrow of Modern Divinity.* Ross-shire, UK: Christian Focus, 2009.

Frame, John. *Systematic Theology: An Introduction to Christian Belief.* Phillipsburg, NJ: P & R Publishing, 2013.

Gentry, Peter and Stephen Wellum. *Kingdom through Covenant: A Biblical-Theological Understanding of the Covenants.* Wheaton, IL: Crossway, 2012.

Golding, Peter. *Covenant Theology: The Key of Theology in Reformed Thought and Tradition.* Glasgow, UK: Mentor, 2004.

Haldane, Robert. *Romans.* Geneva Series of Commentaries. Edinburgh, UK: Banner of Truth Trust, 1996.

Hodge, Charles. *Discussions in Church Polity.* New York, NY: Scribner, 1878.

Hoekema, Anthony. *The Bible and the Future.* Grand Rapids: Eerdmans, 1994.

Hoeksema, Herman. *Believers and Their Seed: Children in the Covenant.* Grand Rapids: Reformed Free Publishing, 1997.

Horton, Michael. *God of Promise: Introducing Covenant Theology.* Grand Rapids: Baker, 2006.

———. *The Christian Faith: A Systematic Theology for Pilgrims on the Way*. Grand Rapids: Zondervan, 2011.

Johnson, Jeffrey D. *The Fatal Flaw of the Theology behind Infant Baptism*. Conway, AR: Free Grace Press, 2010.

Jones, Samuel. *The Doctrine of the Covenants: A Sermon Preached at Pennepeck in Pennsylvania, Sep. 14, 1783*. Philadelphia: F. Bailey, 1783.

Karlberg, Mark W. *Federalism and the Westminster Tradition*. Eugene: Wipf & Stock Publishers, 2006.

Keach, Benjamin. *The Ax Laid to the Root, or, One Blow More at the Foundation of Infant Baptism, and Church Membership*, Part 1. London, UK: B. Keach, 1693.

Kersten, G. H. *Reformed Dogmatics*. 2 vols. Grand Rapids: HeuleGordon, 2009.

Kingdon, David. *Children of Abraham*. Sussex, UK: Carey Publications Ltd., first printed 1973.

Kline, Meredith. *By Oath Consigned*. Grand Rapids: Eerdmans, 1968.

Klink, Edward W. III and Darian R. Lockett. *Understanding Biblical Theology*. Grand Rapids: Zondervan, 2012.

Moo, Douglas. *The Epistle to the Romans*. New International Commentary on the New Testament. Grand Rapids: Eerdmans, 1996.

Murray, John. *The Covenant of Grace*. Phillipsburg, NJ: P & R, 1988.

Owen, John. *An Exposition of the Epistle to the Hebrews*, 7 vols. Carlisle, PA: Banner of Truth Trust, 1991.

———. *Covenant Theology: From Adam to Christ.* Miller, Ronald D., Francisco Orozco, and James M. Renihan, eds. Palmdale, CA: Reformed Baptist Academic Press, 2005.

———. *Biblical Theology.* Morgan, PA: Soli Deo Gloria, 2002.

Owen, John. "Of Infant Baptism and Dipping." in *The Works of John Owen.* 16 vols. Edited by William H. Goold, 1965-1968. Reprint. Edinburgh, UK: Banner of Truth Trust, 2000.

———. "Of Communion with God the Father, Son, and Holy Ghost." *The Works of John Owen.* 16 vols. Edited by William H. Goold, 1965-1968. Reprint. Edinburgh, UK: Banner of Truth Trust, 2000.

Nichols, Greg. *Covenant Theology: A Reformed and Baptistic Perspective on God's Covenants.* Birmingham, AL: Solid Ground Christian Books, 2011.

Petto, Samuel. *The Great Mystery of the Covenant of Grace.* Stoke-on-Trent, UK: Tentmaker Publications, 2007.

Reymond, Robert. *A New Systematic Theology of the Christian Faith.* Nashville: Thomas Nelson Publishers, 1998.

Ridderbos, Herman. *Paul: An Outline of His Theology.* Grand Rapids: Eerdmans, 1975.

———. *The Coming of the Kingdom.* Philadelphia: P & R, 1962.

Robertson, O. Palmer. *The Christ of the Covenants.* Phillipsburg, NJ: P & R Publishing, 1980.

Sanders, E. P. *Paul and Palestinian Judaism.* Philadelphia, PA: Fortress Press, 1977.

Spilsbury, John. *A Treatise Concerning the Lawful Subject of Baptisme.* Reprint. Magazine, AR: The Old Faith Baptist Church, 1993.

Spurgeon, Charles Haddon. *The Sermons of Rev. C. H. Spurgeon of London. 9th Series.* New York, Robert Carter & Brothers, 1883.

Waters, Guy. *The Federal Vision and Covenant Theology: A Comparative Analysis.* Phillipsburg, NJ: P & R, 2006.

Witsius, Herman. *The Economy of the Divine Covenants between God and Man.* Phillipsburg, NJ: P & R, 1990.

Volume 2

Available at
FreeGracePress.com

Other Books by Free Grace Press

The Living Epistle
   by Cornelius Tyree

The Sovereignty of God
   by Jeffrey D. Johnson

God the Preacher and Apologist
   by Lance Quinn

The Exorcism of Satan
   by Joshua P. Howard

Love and Its Fruits: Jonathan Edwards' Charity and Its Fruits, Summarized for the 21st Century
   by Daniel Chamberlin

A Portrait of God: Stephen Charnock's Discourses upon the Existence and Attributes of God, Summarized for the 21st Century
   by Daniel Chamberlin

A Commentary on Galatians
   by Tom Nettles and Sylvia Nettles Dickson

Basic Christian Doctrines
   by Curt Daniel

The Gospel Made Clear to Children
   by Jennifer Adams

Ten Essential Sermons of Charles Spurgeon
   by Charles Spurgeon

Saving Natural Theology from Thomas Aquinas
   by Jeffrey D. Johnson